GW00600784

Also available at all good book stores

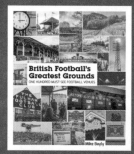

9781785316470

9781785313929

9781785315466

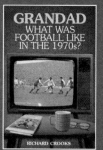

9781785312632

9781785316845

9781785315534

9781785316548

9781785316807

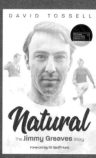

9781785314902

HOME OF ENGLISH FOOTBALL

BOB BOND

HOME OF
ENGLISH FOOTBALL

100 Years
of
Wembley Stadium
in cartoons and caricatures

First published by Pitch Publishing, 2021

Pitch Publishing
A2 Yeoman Gate
Yeoman Way
Worthing
Sussex
BN13 3QZ
www.pitchpublishing.co.uk
info@pitchpublishing.co.uk

© 2021, Bob Bond

Every effort has been made to trace the copyright.
Any oversight will be rectified in future editions at the
earliest opportunity by the publisher.

All rights reserved. No part of this book may be reproduced,
sold or utilised in any form or transmitted in any form or by
any means, electronic or mechanical, including photocopying,
recording or by any information storage and retrieval system,
without prior permission in writing from the Publisher.

A CIP catalogue record is available for this book
from the British Library.

ISBN 978-1-78531-882-5

Typesetting and origination by Pitch Publishing
Printed and bound in India by Replika Press Pvt. Ltd.

Contents

Wembley Stadium

Two words that make the heart beat faster, and bring back to the players and the fans good memories as well as bitter disappointments. Even when you were standing – yes, standing – in the driving wind and rain on a November afternoon, watching a meaningless England game, it was still a magical place to be.

This book will bring back some of those memories of what some people now call the 'good old days'.

Originally built to host the British Empire Exhibition, the old stadium has also been home to the 1948 Olympic Games, rugby league finals, American football occasions, multiple pop concerts, and much more. This book is about football only, with caricature illustrations, rambling reports and, above all, the match cartoons.

The match cartoon was a whole new ball game.
Well, the same ball game really, but a different way of looking at it. The cartoon would appear in Monday's edition of a newspaper, next to the written report of the game. This book is in no way comprehensive. It is simply a selection of the hundreds of football matches to have been played at Wembley. A lot of great games have been missed out, and one or two of little importance are included.

Most of the cartoons were originally drawn in monochrome. Only later have they been enhanced with colour. That doesn't make them any funnier. Some of the later ones were drawn at the time of the event. The earlier ones, of course, have been done in 'retro'. Some of the captions and comments may appear more than once.

Most cartoonists can't recall what they drew ten days ago, let alone ten years. Also this is not a book of statistics, although you might find the odd one here or there.

If you've got this far, read on.

'Wembley is the Cathedral of Football...' Pele

It is now almost 100 years since the original Wembley Stadium was constructed. In 1922 King George V picked up the royal spade and dug up the first sod. Three hundred days later the building of the stadium was completed, which seems remarkably quick. Reports say that it cost £750,000, which seems remarkably cheap – except that money went a lot further back then.

It was built primarily to house the great British Empire Exhibition, planned for 1924, and because of this the new venue was called the Empire Stadium. The work was completed only three days before the first big football match was due to be played there – the 1923 FA Cup Final.

The grandstand and the wooden terraces still had to be safety tested. It must have been quite a sight to see 1,200 men of all shapes and sizes doing synchronised sitting and standing in various places to make sure there could be no collapse of the structure.

'Everybody up; everybody down!'

The two impressive towers were quite a feature of the new stadium, and a trademark. The 'Twin Towers' also became an instantly recognisable nickname. And there were famously the 39 steps for the tired players to climb to the Royal Box to receive their trophy and medals.

Community singing became another feature of FA Cup Final day. The hymn 'Abide With Me' was first sung at the 1927 final. Because Cardiff City were one of the teams involved, 'Land of my Fathers' was sung with even more fervour, and the Welshmen were so inspired that they beat the mighty Arsenal. It was also the first time a commentary of the FA Cup Final was broadcast. To help the unimaginative listener a grid was printed in the *Radio Times*.

As well as the commentary, a voiceover would tell in which part of the field the action was taking place. So originated the expression 'back to square one'.

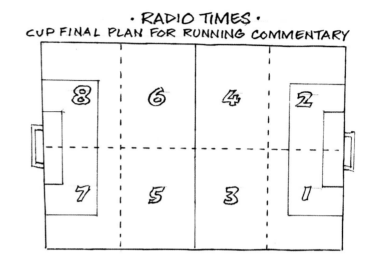

Arthur Caiger, in his famous white suit, became the conductor of the community singing after the Second World War, and continued doing it until 1962.

King George VI only arrived at Wembley after the singing had finished for the day, and asked, 'How did they sing, Arthur?'

'Cracking well, your Majesty!' replied Mr C.

King George added, 'That's good – they've not had very much to sing about lately.'

Depending on the finalists, Arthur had favourite local songs in his repertoire, such as 'She's a Lassie from Lancashire', 'Blaydon Races', 'Ilkley Moor Baht 'at', 'Maybe it's because I'm a Londoner', and many, many more.

In 1963 a new roof was put on the stadium, so now nobody should get wet while watching. And an electronic scoreboard was added, so nobody would have to ask, 'What's the score now, Percy?'

But it was only cosmetic. There was a World Cup coming to England, and the stadium was looking old and tired.

It would have to last another 40 years before anything was done about it.

Meanwhile here are some reminders of the romance that was Wembley.

1923

The Empire Stadium

At last England had a sporting venue fit for an emperor and king. So impressive, and large enough to accommodate everyone who wanted to come and witness any sporting event.

And football had the privilege of being the first such event at this magnificent new arena, with its splendid twin towers, as Bolton Wanderers would play West Ham United in the FA Cup Final.

Bolton were comfortably in the middle of the First Division. Their progress in the cup was courtesy of young David Jack, already one of England's most prolific goalscorers. He had scored the winners in most of Bolton's cup matches, including the only goal in their semi-final against Sheffield United.

West Ham were then only a Second Division side, but knocking on the door of promotion. They'd had a good season, and had scored five times in their semi-final win over Derby County.

Many of their cup goals had been knocked in by Billy Moore. Bring in the fans, bring on the teams.

GEORGE KAY skippered West Ham in this first Wembley final. He had a fine game and was unlucky to be a loser.

Later, as a manager, he led Liverpool to the First Division championship in 1947 and, although a sick man, he returned to Wembley in 1950 to lead out his team in the FA Cup Final. Again he was a loser.

JOE SMITH spent almost all of his playing career with Bolton Wanderers, and was a good enough striker to play for England. He won the FA Cup in 1923 and 1926. Joe also returned to Wembley as a manager, taking Blackpool to three finals, and finally to victory in 1953 – against Bolton.

As everyone soon realised, the Football Association had spectacularly underestimated the interest in the first match at the new Wembley.

Not many advance tickets had been issued, and it was pay at the gate for most fans. While officially 126,000 people paid to get in, many more climbed over gates and turnstiles and entered without paying. It was estimated that close on 200,000 got inside the stadium and spilled off the terraces and on to the pitch itself.

'Clear the pitch, gentlemen. Make room for the players! If you want to see a game, move back please!'

Police Constable George Storey and his horse Billy were the heroes of the day, helping to clear the playing area by pushing people back to the touchline.

As they saw their monarch arrive and sit in his royal seat, the crowd spontaneously burst into 'God Save the King!', and the game began 45 minutes late. David Jack scored the first goal after only two minutes.

The crowd were the touchlines and in many instances the ball bounced back into play off spectators without a throw-in being given!

When John Smith scored the second goal, his shot hit the spectators crammed at the back of the net and rebounded into play. Many of the onlookers thought it had hit a post, but the referee knew it was a goal.

So it was 2-0 to the Wanderers, and King George handed the trophy to Joe Smith, their captain. West Ham consoled themselves by winning promotion.

1928

In 1928 Wembley was the venue for the match with the greatest rivalry of all – England versus Scotland.

It was to be only the second time the countries had met at the new stadium, and when people saw the 11 that Scotland had chosen, it was greeted with a mixture of despair and derision.

The derision was because the tallest of the five Scottish forwards was just 5ft 7in. And many of the players were attached to English clubs anyway, which did not endear them to most Scottish fans. So newspapers north of the border were scathing in their criticism of the selectors.

It became a music hall joke. On stage, comedians asked aloud, 'Would the Scots also be bringing Snow White to go with these vertically challenged men?'

England had chosen a good team, strong and tall and fit, and there was the famous Dixie Dean to knock the goals in. It was difficult to see how they could possibly be beaten.

The day before the game, Scotland's skipper had told his players, 'When you go to bed, pray for rain.'

This was not one of DIXIE DEAN's better days. But how centre halves must have trembled at the prospect of facing Dean at his rampant best. A man who could score 60 goals for his club in one First Division season must have been a fearsome foe.

Dean scored one of Everton's goals against Manchester City in the 1933 FA Cup Final and carried the trophy back to Merseyside afterwards.

But this day at Wembley saw ALEX JAMES at his very best. With his baggy shorts flapping, he toyed with England's ponderous defence. His quick thinking led to him scoring one of Arsenal's goals to win the 1930 final, and he would return to the stadium six years later to skipper the Gunners to another FA Cup success.

You don't have to be tall to be an effective centre-forward, as HUGHIE GALLACHER proved with a record haul of goals for Newcastle, Chelsea and Scotland.

If they did pray, their prayers were answered. The rain made the pitch just that bit slippery, and the wee Scots used the conditions better than England. The home defenders turned slowly, like great ships at sea, and the Scottish forwards were gone with the ball. England might have scored first, Billy Smith smacking his shot against a post. Before he even had time to rue his bad fortune Scotland had broken to the other end with a fast, flowing move, and Alex Jackson had headed a brilliant goal. It was a confidence-booster for the Scots, and they began to pass the ball around as if they owned the place. By contrast England were shaken, and Alex James scored a superb second before half-time. And because the ones he was given were too brief, James had to ask for a pair of his own baggy shorts to be sent for.

Skipper Jimmy McMullan directed operations from midfield, and all those tiny forwards were untouchable. James (two) and Jackson (three) got the goals, but Jimmy Dunn, Alan Morton and Hughie Gallacher were equally excellent.

England's last-minute goal was scant consolation, and they left the slippery field in a daze. Next day the Scottish newspapers were repentant and full of praise for the team they nicknamed the 'Wembley Wizards'.

HERBERT CHAPMAN was the first truly great manager; first with Huddersfield Town, who he led to two First Division championships, and then with Arsenal. When the north London club advertised for a manager in 1925 Chapman applied, knowing that he was the man Arsenal wanted and that this was the job he wanted. He set about strengthening the team, and one of the men he brought in was Charlie Buchan from Sunderland.

When Arsenal reached the FA Cup Final for the first time in 1927, they were firm favourites to beat Cardiff City. But at the very least the Welsh fans standing on the Wembley terraces could sing better than Arsenal's followers. It was the first time community singing had preceded the final. Cardiff must have been inspired by what they were hearing.

But it was a dreadful mistake by the Arsenal goalkeeper that handed the cup to City. And he was a Welshman.

A shot he should have saved comfortably slipped through his fingers and trickled into the net.

So the cup went out of England for the first and only time.

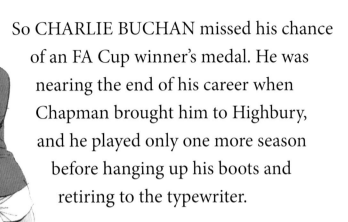

So CHARLIE BUCHAN missed his chance of an FA Cup winner's medal. He was nearing the end of his career when Chapman brought him to Highbury, and he played only one more season before hanging up his boots and retiring to the typewriter.

Chapman wasn't done. He took Arsenal back to Wembley in 1930 where they beat his old team Huddersfield to complete their first FA Cup victory – the first of many.

Not to be outdone, the Germans put in an appearance at the final. The famous Graf Zeppelin airship dipped from the sky and flew over the stadium during the match. Take that, England.

1930

In April 1930 Scotland once more visited Wembley, by which time England had a completely different line-up. Only two players survived the cull. And full-back Fred Goodall and inside-forward Joe Bradford must have had nightmares about the previous embarrassment. Scotland were much changed as well, and sadly for them the replacements were not such wizards.

The result was reversed, as you can see. The surface of the pitch was more to England's liking, and this time they scored first, and proceeded to add three more before half-time.

West Ham's Vic Watson was a successful replacement for Dean and scored two of the goals. Harkness, normally a good and safe goalkeeper, was reduced to a gibbering wreck.

Perhaps, after 1928, the Scots were too confident. Certainly England were hugely determined that it wouldn't happen again. Scotland did better in the second half, but left the arena severely chastened.

In the early 1930s Arsenal, under Chapman, became the outstanding team in the land. Four times they won the First Division title, and when they returned to Wembley for the 1932 FA Cup Final, they had a chance to do the elusive 'double'. But they were the victims of a very controversial goal, and slid to defeat. The ball had quite clearly gone out of play when the Newcastle winger centred for his side's centre-forward to score.

Arsenal were dumbstruck. But the goal stood,

The Magpies went on to win, 2-1. Where is VAR when you need it? At half-time the brass band played a popular tune of the day, 'After the Ball Was Over'.

EDDIE HAPGOOD was one of the great English defenders of the age, and twice left Wembley with an FA Cup winner's medal. For ten years his was the first name to go down on Arsenal's team sheet.

A bust of Herbert Chapman was unveiled, and it became a fixture in the entrance to Highbury.

CLIFF BASTIN's trophy cabinet also had two cup winner's medals. He was a sharpshooting winger who created and scored plenty. For England as well as Arsenal, he had great memories of Wembley.

George Allison succeeded Chapman as manager, and immediately signed TED DRAKE, a centre-forward from Southampton, for £6,000.

In 1936 Drake was seriously injured while playing for England. Arsenal reached the cup final once more, but there were doubts about Drake's fitness. Sheffield United were the opposition. Although not fully fit, Drake did play – and scored the only goal.

1938

Huddersfield Town and Preston North End had contested the FA Cup Final at Stamford Bridge in 1922, the last one to be played before Wembley became the recognised venue.

In that match Preston's goalkeeper wore spectacles, but that didn't help him in the face of the penalty by which Huddersfield won the cup.

Town, under Herbert Chapman would go on to become the team of the 1920s, winning the First Division championship in three consecutive years from 1924 to 1926. By 1938 their heyday was over and Chapman had gone, but they were still a force to be reckoned with. Winger Joe Hulme was playing in his fifth FA Cup Final. The previous four had been for Arsenal.

Preston were no longer proud, either, and certainly not invincible. But they were back at Wembley for the second year running. They had lost to a very good Sunderland side in 1937. Could they reverse the result of 16 years earlier?

And there had not been a penalty in an FA Cup Final since that day.

In 1938 TOM SMITH had good reason to enjoy the thought of going to Wembley. He helped Scotland to beat England 1-0, and then he led out his club Preston North End in the FA Cup Final. A no-nonsense, hard tackling defender, Smith had joined North End from Kilmarnock in 1936.

BILL SHANKLY was another from north of the border who served North End well. He travelled in easy stages from Scotland via Carlisle United before finally arriving in Preston in 1933 for £500.

That would not buy a toenail today, but Shankly played until the war, and after.

He was capped five times for Scotland, and later went back to Wembley as the very successful manager of Liverpool.

It was not quite as dismal a game as the cartoon suggests, but it wasn't a classic either. It was lacking in goalmouth activity, so was not terribly exciting. The midfield ruled, and full-backs hoofed the ball out of danger rather than using it constructively. Then it was hoofed back. You had to have sympathy for the poor football.

For Huddersfield, Boot put the boot in, and Shankly was North End's hard man. Consequently no forward had a clear and obvious chance at goal. Ninety minutes came and went, goalless, and extra time looked like it was going the same way. Neither of the two goalkeepers had been severely tested. As the game entered its final minute the BBC television commentator was heard to say, 'Well, only seconds left now. If anyone scores I'll eat my hat.'

Then, by a curious twist of fate, came a penalty. It was 1922 all over again, and a chance for Preston to avenge what happened. Perhaps neither penalty was clear-cut, but the ball was on the spot.* George Mutch, dazed from his tumble, picked himself up.

'I just closed my eyes and hit it,' he later said. Somewhere a commentator was eating his hat.

*My grandfather, a Preston North End supporter, often told me he was standing behind the goal where Mutch scored the penalty. It hit the underside of the bar before going in.

1946

When football resumed after the hostilities, little had changed. Wembley stadium was the same, unbombed and unscathed, although looking a little tired. The fans, however, had a renewed appetite for football. Back in civilian life and eager to forget the war, they hurried towards the turnstiles in their trilby hats and their demob coats in unprecedented numbers, and wedged themselves into the grounds.

The resumption of the Football League was still a few months away, but the FA Cup set people's hearts racing again. Wembley had staged 'wartime finals', but in May 1946 this was once again the real thing.

Portsmouth had held the FA Cup for seven long years after winning the last final before the war, which brought things to a pause.

Wolves, captained by the great Stan Cullis, were overwhelming favourites that day, but nerves got the better of them and Pompey got the goals. Portsmouth were eliminated early from the 1946 tournament, and had to retrieve the famous trophy from their cellar and hand it back. Derby County had reached the final this time, driven on by their two magical inside-forwards – England's Raich Carter and Irishman Peter Doherty. Carter had already been a cup winner at Wembley in 1937 with Sunderland.

Charlton Athletic lined up on the opposite side of the centre line. The Valley, where they played, would hold almost as many spectators as Wembley itself, and often over 60,000 would assemble to watch Charlton play. Their goalkeeper was Sam Bartram, as brilliant as he was eccentric. More of Sam later, but this final was billed as the battle of the redheads – Doherty and Bartram.

Some 100,000 packed the stadium that day, simply glad to be back 'proper' – and for the million listeners at home there was Raymond Glendenning on the steam radio barking out the news that 'STAMPS HAS SCORED!'

It certainly turned out to be an entertaining affair, and many experts nominated it as the 'best Wembley final so far'.

When Portsmouth's JIMMY GUTHRIE lifted the FA Cup at Wembley after a shock defeat of Wolves in 1939, he couldn't have imagined it would be seven years before he had to hand it back!

Irishman PETER DOHERTY's best years were before the war, when he won a First Division championship with Manchester City. Conversely he then experienced relegation with them the following season. His first English club had been Blackpool.

The 1946 final was the only time Peter played at Wembley. Later that year he left Derby after a disagreement with the directors.

He did return to Wembley as manager of the Northern Ireland team who won a memorable victory over England in 1957 (see page 74).

Yes, Jack Stamps did score – twice – in extra time, but he was merely decorating the cake that had been baked and iced by Doherty, who was head and shoulders above anyone else on the Wembley field. But for nearly all of the 90 minutes he and his fellow attackers were frustrated by Charlton's resolute defence, and by Bartram's safe goalkeeping.

Derby did most of the pressing, and deserved their eventual victory. Bartram's goal stayed intact until Turner inadvertently deflected Duncan's shot into his own net. Only five minutes remained. But Derby had no time to celebrate as immediately Charlton won a free kick, and Turner atoned for his own goal.

So an extra half-hour was needed. It was then that Derby took the game by the scruff of the neck. Having won his personal scrap with Bartram when he fired his side back in front, Doherty then set up the two late goals for Stamps.

AND STAMPS HAS SCORED!' screamed the commentator...

The rivalry between England and Scotland on any battlefield is legendary, so there was mounting anticipation of the renewal of this contest for superiority.

Scotland had not been beaten at Wembley since 1934. Indeed the Scots had the better record in these clashes – 29 victories to England's paltry 19.

England chose the experienced Stanley Matthews rather than the younger Tom Finney on the right wing, even though the Preston man had scored in three of his first four internationals. It was a question of seniority and clearly the correct thing to do. And when God gave out the good looks, England's captain must have been at the front of the queue.

Wembley was ready, the sun was shining, and the gloves were on.

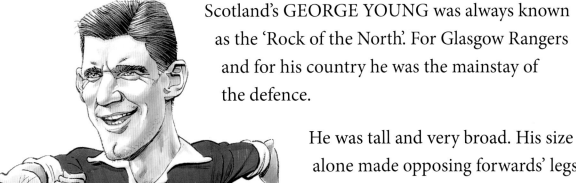

Scotland's GEORGE YOUNG was always known as the 'Rock of the North'. For Glasgow Rangers and for his country he was the mainstay of the defence.

He was tall and very broad. His size alone made opposing forwards' legs turn to jelly. They thought twice before going for a 50/50 ball with Young, yet he was entirely fair. He was equally comfortable at centre-half or full-back.

He made 53 appearances for Scotland and loved playing at Wembley where he was only on the losing side once in five outings.

FRANK SWIFT was a giant of a goalkeeper. His first experience of Wembley was as a young man who overcame his nerves to defy Portsmouth and help Manchester City to win the FA Cup in 1934. As the final whistle signalled a famous City win, Swift spun around and fainted.

He later appeared several times for England at Wembley.

Some 98,000 people watched the game on a warm April afternoon. Perhaps the temperature was too warm, for it was a rather turgid affair. If the fans expected a feast of football, all they got was a stale sandwich. Neither side could string many passes together.

Walter Winterbottom was England's new manager after the war, and he had some of the greatest footballers of all time at his disposal. But Walter didn't pick the team.

This was done by committee, and every committee member had his own agenda, his own favourite players and the ones he didn't like. So not always was the best team put on the field. And not always the team that Walter would have chosen.

Sometimes the England team-mates would meet each other for the first time in the dressing room before the match! Scotland knew each other a little better.

England's shooting rarely threatened the Scottish goalposts. Scotland were a goal ahead at half-time, deservedly. Hard-as-nails Jimmy Delaney, normally a winger, was chosen at centre-forward for Scotland, and gave Neil Franklin a rough time.

But Raich Carter, playing at Wembley for the last time, equalised, and might have won it but for a mysterious whistle. Non, the referee Monsieur Delasalle from France hadn't blown it. The man in the crowd who had done had probably had enough of a disappointing game.

In 1947 there were shortages and ration books. There was a concern for children being undernourished.

But after so many years of austerity, people longed to be entertained. Cinema audiences were at an all-time high, and when the Football League was resumed huge crowds made their way on to the terraces, the demobbed in their mackintoshes and those waiting to be demobbed still in their khaki, but desperate to see some football. The years after the war were considered by many as the sport's 'golden age'.

It was a time of spectacular action. Every team seemed to have its celebrated hero – Stanley Matthews at Blackpool, Tom Finney at Preston, Tommy Lawton at Chelsea, Wilf Mannion at Middlesbrough, and Sam Bartram at Charlton.

And Wembley waited for the big occasions; international matches and the FA Cup Final. In April 1947 Charlton were back there once more, on merit, having thrashed Newcastle in their semi-final in Leeds. Bartram was one of only five men who had survived from the previous year's defeat. Don Welsh, with the fast receding hairline, scored twice against Newcastle, and captained the side.

Their opponents were Burnley, a Second Division team but set for promotion to the top division. It was too close to call. Wembley was looking its best, and once again 100,000 fans waited and wondered.

Only one thing appeared certain. The ball couldn't possibly burst for the second consecutive year – could it?

After the previous year, the game itself was a dour affair.

SAM BARTRAM was probably the best goalkeeper never to be chosen to play for England. This was the mercurial Sam's fourth successive cup final at Wembley; as well as appearing in the previous year's encounter he had played in the last two Football League War Cup Finals – for Charlton and for Millwall.

A one-club man in peacetime, Bartram made 623 appearances for Charlton.

Charlton's BERT JOHNSON was a steady wing-half who never had a bad game, and enjoyed his every minute on the pitch – especially if it was a mud-heap.

So, the ball did deflate after all. It's a good job it did, because it awoke the crowd from its slumber, so little else was there to excite them in the first 90 goalless minutes. Burnley's solid defence, which had been the backbone of their promotion challenge, had nullified Charlton's tricky forwards. Wembley baked in the hot sunshine.

The spectators also sweated, eager for a goal to cheer. Players puffed and blowed. Not all footballers returning from military service were as fit as they would have liked to have been. The half-time and full-time whistles were a welcome sound, signalling time for a sit down, a drink, and a sneaky cigarette.

Bartram had very little to extend himself for. Kippax, Burnley's amateur left-winger of whom so much was expected, was completely shut out of the game by Croker, the best player on the field.

It looked like the game was heading for a replay when Duffy lit up the dreary proceedings with his stunning finish. It was a custard pie in the face of Burnley.

1948

The approaching 1948 FA Cup showpiece was awaited more eagerly than any previous final. It brought together two of the most charismatic teams in the land, and for both of them it was their first time at Wembley.

Manchester United's new manager had assembled a team that played fast, flowing football and scored goals freely. They had an inspiring and commanding captain in Irishman Johnny Carey.

United's defence could be breached, but they had the popular philosophy that if the opposition scored three, they would get four.

In an earlier round Aston Villa had scored four against them, but even that wasn't enough to prevent United winning.

Blackpool was everyone's favourite seaside town, with its Golden Mile and fortune tellers, its famous illuminations, its Winter Gardens, zoo, circus, three piers and its fish and chips. And of course, the Blackpool Tower.

And they were everyone's favourite other team. Because they, too, played attractive football – and they had the great Stanley Matthews, the 'Wizard of the Dribble', who deserved, if anyone did, to add an FA Cup winner's medal to his trophy cabinet.

Wembley, bedecked with flags, waited expectantly. And the 1948 final didn't disappoint.

MATT BUSBY was the young manager of Manchester United in 1948, happy to put his boots back on and join in his new club's training routines. Old Trafford had been badly damaged by wartime bombing, so he had to do a lot of reorganising with the rebuilding of a stadium as well as rebuilding a competitive team.

Busby had been a Wembley winner as a player – with Manchester City in 1934 – and was a good enough half-back to play for Scotland.

He also made hundreds of appearances for Liverpool before the war broke out.

Bandy-legged JIMMY DELANEY had gained a Scottish Cup winner's medal with Celtic 11 years previously, and was on his way to a unique treble – adding English and Irish cup wins to his CV. He would play in any forward position you asked him to.

MAN UNITED 4
BLACKPOOL 2

IT APPEARS THAT THE PATHE NEWS CAMERAMAN FELL ASLEEP AND MISSED UNITED'S FOURTH GOAL.

THE PHOTOGRAPHERS BESIDE THE GOAL ALL MISSED IT TOO. SO HERE IT COMES IN SLOW MOTION CARTOON.

THE ANDERSON SHOT...

THE WICKED RICOCHET FROM A BLACKPOOL DEFENDER...

...AND BEFORE YOU COULD SAY JOE ROBINSON IT WAS IN THE NET.

JACK ROWLEY, WHO NETTED UNITED'S TWO EQUALISERS BEFORE STAN PEARSON PUT THEM AHEAD.

BY GENERAL CONSENT IT WAS A GREAT FINAL, WITH THE LOSERS PLAYING THEIR PART. JOE SMITH KNOWS WHAT IT'S LIKE TO WIN HERE AS A PLAYER.

HE VOWS HE'LL BE BACK TO WIN THE F.A. CUP AS A MANAGER.

THROUGHOUT IT ALL ALLENBY CHILTON'S CENTRE PARTING STAYED IN PLACE...

...AS DID JOHNNY ASTON'S CHIN DIMPLE.

JOHNNY CAREY RECEIVED THE CUP FROM THE KING WITH A MIXTURE OF NOBILITY AND HUMILITY.

It was universally agreed that this was the best FA Cup Final at Wembley so far. It did Wembley proud but, as often before, the final had its controversial moments.

Soon after the start, Blackpool's Mortensen raced through, only to be brought down from behind by a last desperate tackle. Perhaps the tackle was outside the penalty box, but Mortensen fell inside, and the referee pointed to the spot. In 2020 it would also have been a sending off, but not then.

Blackpool scored from the resulting penalty. United then equalised, but Mortensen soon reclaimed the lead. He was the Seasiders' other Stanley, and was certainly on fire.

In the second half United gradually achieved supremacy. They had their own free-scoring centre-forward, Jack Rowley, and his second goal put the game right back in the melting pot.

Stan Pearson – how many Stanleys do you need? – scored an excellent goal following a flowing, length-of-the-field move, and Matt's men won it deservedly after their strong comeback. As the cartoon showed, the news cameraman on whom we depended to record all the goals, didn't meet those expectations.

1949

You have to love Leicester City, don't you? When they won the Premier League title in 2016, there was universal rejoicing, and that success can never be erased from the record books.

In 1949 they went unexpectedly to the FA Cup Final for the first time. City were only a Second Division side, but had surprisingly beaten the First Division champions Portsmouth in the semi-final. But they would have to play without young Don Revie, in hospital with a burst blood vessel. Revie had scored twice against Portsmouth and would be missed.

Their opponents were Wolves, firm favourites but themselves without an FA Cup Final victory since 1908. They were festooned with star players. Young Billy Wright was their captain, and he had also recently been made captain of England. All this was long before he found Joy with a Beverley Sister.

Bert Williams was a sometimes spectacular but always safe goalkeeper. And they had two speedy wingers in Jimmy Mullen and Johnny Hancocks, a diminutive man with small boots which packed a thunderous shot. There was also sharpshooter Jesse Pye.

So the City fans made the trip to Wembley, second favourites of course. Those same fans would get used to this. Three more times in the next 20 years they would make the same journey, full of hope. Every time they returned to Leicester, their dreams were in tatters.

Like Busby, STAN CULLIS won more silverware as a manager than he did as a player. Mighty fine wing-half as he was, capped by England and skipper of a good Wolves team just before and after the war, he had two major disappointments. Wolves, though overwhelming favourites, lost the final in 1939, and also the First Division championship was snatched from them in 1947 when they lost their last match at Molineux to Liverpool, who took the title.

Cullis was appointed manager of Wolves a year later and under his guidance three First Division championships were won, and this was the first of two FA Cup wins.

BERT WILLIAMS was a spectacular goalkeeper for Wolves and England in the years after the war.

So, as the cartoon shows, Leicester did lose. But of course, being Wembley, the match had to have its moment of controversy. City had given themselves a mountain to climb in the second half, but were going about it pretty well. They scored one goal, and Wolves were clearly rattled. Leicester thought they had the equaliser, too, and quite possibly if they'd had VAR then the referee's offside decision would have been overturned.

Leicester were still arguing with referee Mr Mortimer when Sammy Smyth waltzed through their defence to score one of Wembley's great solo goals and put an end to the revival.

Beaten but not humiliated, the Foxes returned home to get on with the job of avoiding relegation to the Third Division. This they did in spite of a few more Jelly wobbles.

As for Revie, he would return to Wembley and be on the winning side both as player and as manager.

1951 and 1952

In the early 1950s Wembley belonged to Newcastle United.

'Why, mon – it's our second home groond,' boasted their fans. The song 'Blaydon Races' echoed around St James' Park and many other famous arenas – and Wembley – as in the cup Newcastle carried all before them.

A well-known radio programme of the day was 'In Town Tonight' – the town being London. On cup final day Newcastle and their followers were very often 'in town'.

They may not have challenged for league honours, but the FA Cup seemed to lift them to special heights. Newcastle had all the men for the job.

Joe Harvey, the inspiring captain, with Frank Brennan and Jimmy Scoular made up a take-no-prisoners half-back line.

Skilful Ernie Taylor was a pocket dynamo at inside-forward, and on the left wing was Scotland's Bobby Mitchell.

In the 1952 semi-final replay Newcastle were having a difficult time disposing of Blackburn Rovers before being awarded a late penalty.

'Give us the ball – I'll tek it!' said Bobby, as everyone else dithered.

Ice-cool, he drove his shot into the net like a bullet from a gun.

Blackpool, once again with Stanley Matthews looking for a winner's medal to crown a brilliant career, were Newcastle's opponents in 1951.

Arsenal faced them in the 1952 final.

JACKIE MILBURN was the one the Newcastle fans pinned most of their hopes upon. He repaid them with three goals in three Wembley finals, and was one of three men – Cowell and Mitchell being the others – to come back with three winner's medals.

Milburn made eight international appearances for England at a time when there was much competition for the number nine shirt.

JOE MERCER had captained Arsenal to a convincing FA Cup Final victory over Liverpool in 1950. The Gunners played in gold shirts that day, as this picture shows.

Joe had joined Arsenal in 1946. Although his return to Wembley two years later ended in defeat, Arsenal left the field with their heads held high.

Blackpool lost and still Stanley Matthews, possibly football's greatest player, awaited that ultimate decoration of a brilliant career. Was this his last chance?

The Seasiders would look back on the key moments of a splendid game, and think 'if only'.

If only, in the first half, Bobby Cowell had not appeared from nowhere to clear Mortensen's header off the Newcastle goal line with goalkeeper Fairbrother stranded.

If only Blackpool had not got their offside strategy wrong when Newcastle scored their first goal. While defenders stood with arms out wide, looking for the linesman's flag, Milburn was away. Just onside when Robledo's pass was made, Wor Jackie raced on, uncatchable, and drove the ball past the advancing Farm.

Blackpool could do nothing about Milburn's second. It was just as the cartoon depicted, only much, much better than that, and 2-0 was the right result in the end.

Newcastle bossed the second half, 'Blaydon Races' rang around the stadium, and Joe Harvey was over the moon to receive the cup from King George.

NEWCASTLE 1 ARSENAL 0

Newcastle won the cup again, but this time most of the plaudits went to the losers.

Arsenal had to contend with misfortune when their Welsh international full-back twisted his knee when his studs stuck in the turf. Barnes, unable to continue, limped off. It was the first time the Wembley injury hoodoo had struck, but it was certainly not going to be the last*.

As Arsenal's ten men fought on, fitness and stamina began to tell. Players in red dropped to their knees. Mercer, no spring chicken himself, did his utmost to rally his troops.

As the cartoon shows, Lishman's overhead effort so nearly found its mark.

Arthur Ellis was the man in charge, and the most respected whistler of his day. He was later to find even greater fame as a referee on *It's a Knockout!*

When Arsenal's Roper fell down, injured, Arthur could have stopped the game, but instead allowed play to proceed. A few seconds later, via Robledo's head, the ball was in Swindin's net. Arsenal were on their knees, the bravest of all Wembley losers.

*Seven times in ten years teams would have to battle on in FA Cup Finals with only ten men. The Wembley grass was blamed by some. Cramp, too, was a regular visitor late in games.

1953

It was a momentous year. Queen Elizabeth II was crowned, and a million new television sets had been purchased in the weeks leading up to her coronation. On those same sets people would hear the news that at long last Everest had been conquered, and they watched other events unfold. Gordon Richards, the world's most famous jockey, winning the Derby for the first (and last) time on Pinza, England winning back the Ashes from Australia after many barren years.

Of course Wembley could not be kept out of all this jollity, and would put on a showpiece of an FA Cup Final – the best and the most dramatic so far.

Blackpool were here again, for the third time in six years. Their earlier finals had ended in defeat, but you had to admire their perseverance. The whole nation was agog.

Unless you came from Bolton, you hoped that this time Stanley Matthews would collect that elusive winner's medal from the new Queen and everyone could rejoice with him. One of the teams that Blackpool had beaten on the way was Arsenal, at Highbury, but not without cost. Allan Brown, their Scottish international inside-forward had tragically broken a leg in the act of scoring the winning goal. So he would have to miss the final – the second time this had happened to him.

Bolton were Blackpool's opponents.

This all-Lancashire final had everything – mistakes, goals, passion and drama, all building up to a storybook ending. Bolton took the lead in the second minute when Farm should have saved Lofthouse's shot. But his confidence wasn't helped by a nervous defence. And vice-versa.

Mortensen, as often before, came to Blackpool's rescue, and his shot was deflected past Hanson, who went down slowly and heavily. He looked like he'd had too many chips for his dinner. So two nervous goalkeepers added to the uncertainty of what would happen next. Another weak flap by Farm at a cross led to Moir's head putting Bolton in front again. And this with only ten fit men, for wing-half Bell had become another victim of the Wembley jinx. Limping badly, Bell could still be a nuisance and unbelievably headed Bolton 3-1 ahead. With barely 20 minutes left, it was now or never for Blackpool and for Matthews.

This match has become known as the 'Matthews Final', but the Seasiders would not have won without Mortensen. He squeezed the ball into Bolton's net after Hanson had only waved goodbye at a Matthews centre to bring the score back to 3-2. Mortensen's equaliser was the best goal of the day – a blistering free kick with only a square foot to aim at and with barely a minute left on the clock.

But there was still time enough, and Bolton's defence was now standing still. We all knew at that moment that Blackpool would win. Matthews took the ball to the byline again and rolled it across to his waiting forwards. 'Hit that,' he said, 'and give me my medal.'

In 1953, First Division footballers could earn £14 a week during the playing season and £10 a week for not doing anything in the summer months. Not all the players received quite the same.

A few star players like Matthews, Wright and Finney were paid a little more than the plodders and hoofers. Tommy Docherty once asked his club, Preston North End, if they could see their way to paying him as much as they paid Finney, who got more in the playing season and in the close season.

'But you're not as good as Finney,' he was told. 'I am in the summer,' said Doc.

Here's a match when the two Toms unusually faced each other playing for their different countries. England also had two Froggatts, Jack and Redfern, on the left of their attack. They were cousins.

England had played Scotland three times since the war, and had not won any of them. Would the 1953 encounter end this disappointing sequence?

TOM FINNEY's one disappointment was not winning the FA Cup with Preston North End in 1954 when his team lost to West Brom. Finney was not 100 per cent fit that day, but he was pushed into playing.

He often performed brilliantly at Wembley, where he played on either wing for England, and at centre-forward. Tom was the complete professional, and a gentleman both on and off the field.

LAURIE REILLY loved playing at Wembley, where he was often the one player England forgot to mark. He scored on four visits, only one of which Scotland lost.

'When you're leading 2-1 with only a minute of the game left, kick it anywhere. Over the stand if you can. Just don't let the ball come near your goal.'

England forgot this fundamental rule when they allowed the ever-prowling Reilly to equalise for Scotland in the dying seconds. Reilly had now scored four times against England at Wembley, where the Scots had not lost since 1934.

Their spirit and courage deserved nothing less than a draw, for they had to play the last 20 minutes with only ten men. The visitors began better, and it was rather against the run of play when England took the lead midway through the first half, Finney sending Broadis through with a perfect pass. The home defence had some amazing escapes before and after the interval. Merrick must have supped from some magic potion which helped to keep his goal intact, especially when Steel thwacked his crossbar. When Johnstone did the same thing it seemed like the ball would simply not go in, but Reilly forced in the rebound to equalise. It was end-to-end stuff now, and Finney sped past Cox to lay on a second goal for Broadis. In trying to stop the Preston man, Cox was left writhing in agony, and could take no further part.

It seemed like curtains for Scotland, but they refused to give in and with 30 seconds remaining Reilly beat Merrick to give the result the right appearance.

England had been beaten on their own soil frequently by Scotland, and very occasionally by Wales and Northern Ireland. Once, at Goodison Park, the Republic of Ireland had turned them over. But they had never been beaten here by a country from outside the British Isles.

There was a certain preciousness about this record, and a feeling that it might last forever. A combined Rest of the World team, in an exciting 4-4 draw at the stadium, had given an indication that other countries were catching up. But that hardly counted. Wembley was a fortress to be stormed occasionally, but never surrendered lightly.

Hungary, therefore, when they arrived at headquarters on a grey, misty day in November 1953, had a mountain of reputation to overcome. They would be fearful, surely, and probably faint right away.

The word was that the Hungarians were a very fast and skilful side. They were Olympic champions after all. But England were solid and well organised, relying on those time-honoured qualities which had always seen them through in the past. And there was always Matthews, back on the very field where he had destroyed Bolton Wanderers a few months earlier. A comfortable England win was expected.

Those of us old enough can remember exactly where we were when we heard the result from Wembley that day.

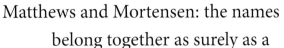

Matthews and Mortensen: the names belong together as surely as a horse and carriage. STAN MORTENSEN was the goalscorer – over 200 for Blackpool and lots more for England. Wembley frequently saw Mortensen at his best, with an FA Cup Final hat-trick top of his chart hits.

ERNIE TAYLOR played only once for England, and was unlucky to choose this day, where he was completely upstaged by the Magical Magyars. Taylor played for three different clubs in FA Cup Finals, and was twice a winner.

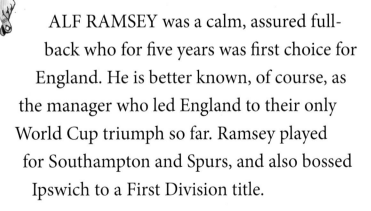

ALF RAMSEY was a calm, assured full-back who for five years was first choice for England. He is better known, of course, as the manager who led England to their only World Cup triumph so far. Ramsey played for Southampton and Spurs, and also bossed Ipswich to a First Division title.

So, inside the bowl that was Wembley Stadium, the inevitable finally happened, and England were beaten by a foreign invader for the first time.

It little mattered to the Magyars that it was a misty day. Long before the end, it was England who were in a fog. To those who had sensed that the best continental teams were creeping closer to the high standard set by England, this was no real surprise. It was the size of the score that shocked.

As one of the Hungarians was performing amazing keepy-uppies with a ball, there were astonished looks on some English faces. And the game hadn't even kicked off yet. When it did, England were chasing shadows. Hidegkuti fired into the roof of Merrick's net after just two minutes.

Jackie Sewell, an excellent inside-forward who had deserved his selection, equalised. That was more like it. But if we thought things were getting better, they soon got worse, far worse. From then on the white shirts were cut to ribbons by some of the most fluent football we had ever seen.

The Hungarians moved the ball mesmerically with short and long passes, changing the direction of their attacks at speed, and finished clinically.

Three goals quickly followed, including that masterly finish by Puskas, the brightest of all the stars on view.

There was still half an hour to go when Hidegkuti hit his third and his team's sixth. Those watching with a mixture of horror and admiration wondered what the final score might be. Thankfully the Hungarians eased up after that.

England found out that it's never easy to win a football match when the opposition won't let you have the ball.

1955

Len Shackleton became known as the 'Clown Prince of Soccer'. It was a perfect description of a player capable of doing amazing things with a football, entertaining the terraces and clearly enjoying every moment on the pitch. Off the pitch he could be controversial.

Len played for England only five times, which was an insult to his skill. One of these appearances was against West Germany, then world champions in 1954, when he scored one of the most impudent goals ever seen at Wembley. But too much of an individualist for the selectors, he never played for England again.

The following year, when Scotland came south for the annual test of strength, the number ten shirt was worn by Dennis Wilshaw, less of an entertainer than Shack, but a deadly finisher.

Duncan Edwards, Manchester United's powerful wing-half, was making his international debut at 18 years old – the youngest England player ever.

DUNCAN EDWARDS was the finest young player ever to pull on an England shirt. He perished in the terrible Munich air crash in 1958 which robbed Manchester United and England of some wonderful players. Had Edwards lived, there would have been no room for Bobby Moore in the number six shirt of England.

NAT LOFTHOUSE enjoyed playing at Wembley, and was a frequent goalscorer there for his club Bolton Wanderers and for England. For a time, he shared with Finney the England scoring record – until Jimmy Greaves came along. Nat was a loser in the 1953 final, but a winner in 1958 when he got both of Bolton's goals.

DENNIS WILSHAW's appearances at Wembley were only for England, but in this match he was deadly Dennis. Only a handful of men have scored four or more goals in a match at HQ.

With their first victory over Scotland at Wembley for 21 years, England finally laid to rest the hoodoo – with a vengeance!

The 96,000 crowd included many Scottish supporters with their tartan favours, but it wasn't long before the England followers were cheering the first goal. Scotland goalkeeper Martin made the first of several blunders and Wilshaw fired the ball home.

As the cartoon opposite depicts, 40-year-old Matthews gave Haddock a torrid time, and soon laid on a second goal for Lofthouse. Reilly, who always scored at Wembley, reduced the lead from Johnstone's pass, but before half-time England had pulled clear with more goals from Revie and Lofthouse.

There was now no way back for the Scots. Young Duncan Edwards looked a tremendous prospect, while in the last 20 minutes Wilshaw scored three more times. With his head and both feet he demonstrated some of the finishing power he had been showing for Wolves in the league.

Even as the score mounted, Docherty continued to work tirelessly for Scotland and deserved his goal, a fiercely struck free kick past Williams.

The England selectors acknowledged Chelsea's winning of the First Division championship by picking Ken Armstrong* who gave a sound display at wing-half.

*It was Armstrong's only England appearance. He later emigrated to New Zealand for whom he won 13 caps.

1956

It had been over two years since England had been put to the sword by the Hungarians, and a few lessons had been learned. The shorts were shorter and the boots lighter. Some bright young players had emerged and some oldies pensioned off. Of the forward line that had demolished Scotland 7-2 just a year earlier, only the ageing Stanley Matthews kept his place. Roger Byrne, Duncan Edwards and Tommy Taylor were three of Matt Busby's babes on whom future hopes were being pinned.

And there was a different challenge, this time from the gifted South Americans of Brazil. The match was billed as 'The Old World meets the New'. Brazil were not yet the power in the world they were to become, but they were skilful enough to attract a capacity crowd to Wembley on a Wednesday afternoon. Once again the excitement and the anticipation was rising, almost tangible. The whole world recognised the great Nilton Santos, and his direct clash with Matthews was eagerly awaited.

Greatness opposed to greatness, although neither was in the first flush of youth.

We knew that Brazil could also be temperamental and easily provoked into doing stupid things, and that might be their downfall. The French referee might have his hands full.

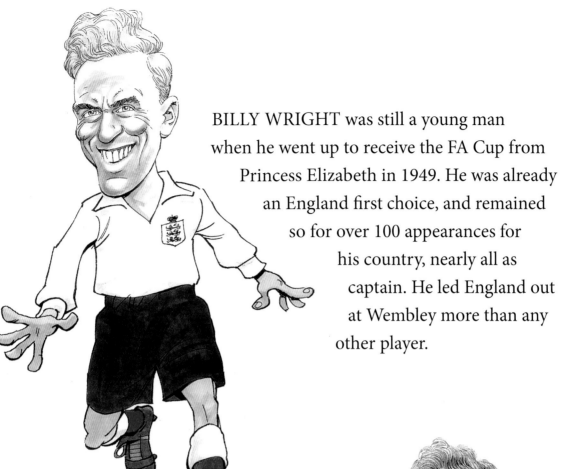

BILLY WRIGHT was still a young man when he went up to receive the FA Cup from Princess Elizabeth in 1949. He was already an England first choice, and remained so for over 100 appearances for his country, nearly all as captain. He led England out at Wembley more than any other player.

ROY BENTLEY scored twice for Chelsea in a semi-final in 1950, but was still on the losing side. It was the closest he got to an FA Cup Final. But he did score a hat-trick for England at Wembley, against Wales in 1954.

It was a thoroughly entertaining game, and England were quickly out of the starting blocks. Taylor justified his inclusion immediately with a goal inside two minutes, smashing a lovely pass from Haynes into the roof of Brazil's net, and Colin Grainger marked his debut with a second goal a few minutes later. Stanley Matthews was giving Nilton Santos a torrid time. Brazil were clearly shaken, but slowly eased their way into the match with some flowing moves. When Paulinho scored just after the interval it was England's turn to panic. The other Matthews – goalkeeper Reg – should have saved Didi's shot which made it 2-2. With the game in the melting pot that crazy moment arrived. The cartoon opposite doesn't fully explain the incident. A free kick was awarded to England which, with the referee's consent, Haynes took quickly. 'Too quickly,' thought Santos, who caught the ball and handed it back to Haynes.

'Handball,' decreed the referee, and a penalty was awarded.

Pandemonium ensued as a Brazilian defender walked away with the ball and refused to return it. Order was eventually restored and the penalty was taken. And not surprisingly missed. England did finally get the goals that won the game, both Taylor and Grainger netting for the second time. In between, another penalty was missed, saved by Gilmar.

So ended one of Wembley's more eventful games. It was a successful debut for Sheffield United's Grainger, meaning he could also give up his nightclub singing career if he wished.

1957

'Ish thish Wembley?'

'No, ish Thursday.'

'Sho am I. Letsh have a drink.'

Everyone is familiar with the James Balmforth postcard showing two rather tipsy, red-nosed gentlemen, bedecked with football scarves, sitting on a train as it pulls into a station. And we all think we know the exact people that these men were modelled on.

This was Wembley, and England were playing Northern Ireland this time, in a regulation Home International. And a regulation home victory was expected. The Irish had won only once in England, and that was before Wembley was even thought of. Unusually England had neither Matthews nor Finney on the wings, so perhaps this was the opportunity for the Irish to break their duck.

Ireland had a wealth of experience in their side with Blanchflower brothers, Danny and Jackie, at half-back. In attack they could play Bingham, McIlroy and McParland, all stars of the English First Division.

Their goalkeeper was Harry Gregg, then of Doncaster Rovers, but soon to be a Manchester United player.

JIMMY McILROY was a clever inside-forward for Burnley, appearing in the 1962 FA Cup Final against Spurs, when his colleague Danny Blanchflower left with the trophy.

Like McIlroy, PETER McPARLAND would always remember with affection Northern Ireland's match against England at Wembley in 1957. But McParland also gained a cup winner's medal at Wembley the following year when he scored the two goals for Villa in their victory over Manchester United.

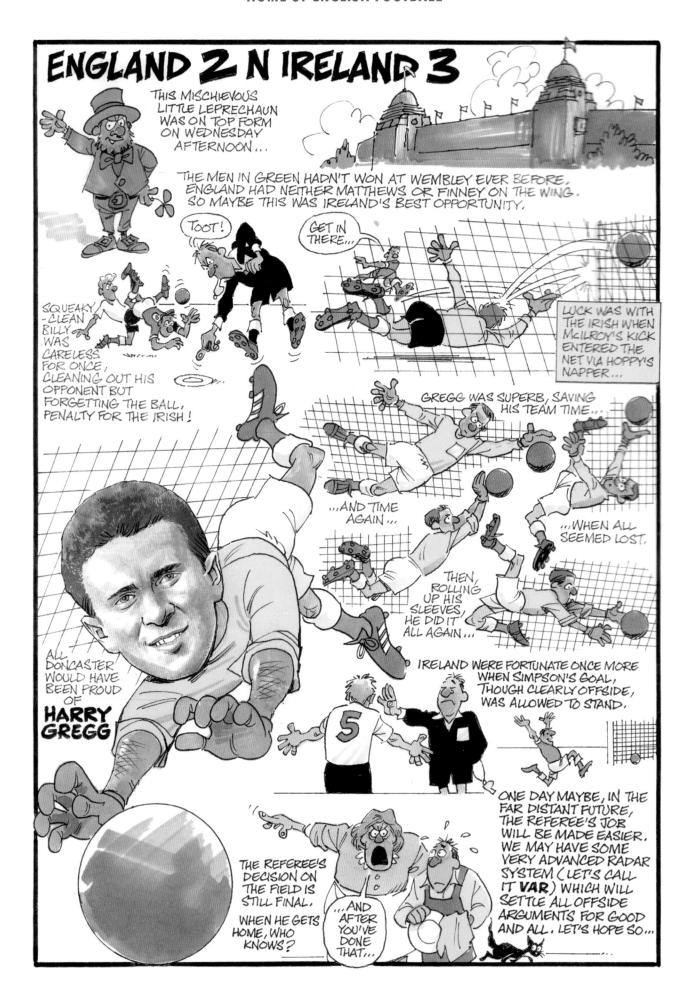

Only 42,000 were present at Wembley to see Northern Ireland's historic win.

And for a long time it simply didn't look likely as England began better, with Haynes particularly prominent with his incisive passing. It appeared just a matter of time before their superiority would turn to goals. But the Welsh referee deemed that Wright's tackle on McGrory was a foul, and McIlroy's penalty kick found its fortuitous way into England's net.

A mixture of bad luck – England struck the woodwork twice – and some brilliant goalkeeping by Gregg kept Ireland in front at half-time.

Alan A'Court, on his international debut, equalised with a snap shot, and surely England would go on to win.

Within a minute McGrory's shot went in off a post, and the surprise was back on. If the goalposts were England's bugbear, they were Ireland's friend. Again referee Griffiths was on the side of the Irish when Simpson headed in Bingham's cross from what looked suspiciously like an offside position.

All England's pleadings were in vain. Edwards* thumped in a great goal, but Gregg saved everything else and was chaired off at the end by the jubilant Irish supporters.

'Ish thish Wembley?'

It certainly was, and the fans could be forgiven if they enjoyed a few drinks afterwards.

*We didn't know it at the time, of course, but Roger Byrne, Duncan Edwards and Tommy Taylor would play only once more for England before losing their lives in that terrible air crash in Munich.

1960

Spain paraded six of the famous Real Madrid team for this friendly international at Wembley in October 1960. Real, of course, had been winners of the European Cup in every one of the five years since its inception.

Gento was their express train on the left wing. Would Jimmy Armfield be able to keep up with him? Del Sol was an elusive and deadly striker, while the great Di Stefano, creator and playmaker, had been a goalscorer in each of those five finals. The thought could be so frightening.

But England had reason to hope. This was their third match in a month, the first two having brought them 14 goals and a settled attack which was firing on all cylinders.

Bobby Smith was playing in only his third England game and was looking like the complete centre-forward. He had already scored 14 league goals as his Spurs team was storming away towards a certain First Division championship.

BRYAN DOUGLAS had a wonderful game against Spain, as he so often did for England at Wembley. He was a goalscoring winger for Blackburn Rovers. His only FA Cup Final appearance was spoiled by the return of the injury bogeyman, leaving Rovers with a hopeless task against Wolves in 1960.

In that prolific-scoring England team of 1960 BOBBY ROBSON played an important role as an attacking wing-half. But it is for his spell as his country's manager that Robson is better remembered, and especially for the near-miss of Italia 90.

Weather-wise, it was an appalling day of wild wind and driving rain. A crowd of 80,000 braved the elements and were rewarded with an England performance that warmed the very cockles of the heart. Spain's superstars were finally sent to defeat, but not before Suarez and his team had battled bravely from start to finish. The way England kept possession of the ball in the closing minutes with some delightful passing and moving for the return pass was something we had never seen from them before. The Spaniards had a taste of their own medicine. England had notched 18 goals in three games in the month of October, and now appeared to have an attack that could score almost at will.

They scored a goal in the first minute. A fine move down the right wing between Douglas and Smith ended with Greaves bursting through the rain and mud and flailing defenders and driving a low shot beyond Ramallets. It was just the start that England and the fans wanted.

But Spain were up for the challenge, and Del Sol equalised after a lovely move. The slippery conditions helped to make it a fast, exciting game, and Douglas headed England back in front from Armfield's perfect centre. It was a deserved half-time lead.

Of course Spain were not done, and back they came once more with a goal from Suarez for 2-2, and England had to begin again. Roared on by their home supporters they took the lead for a third time, Smith heading in Charlton's cross. Then came the sublime moment from big, burly Bobby Smith. Dragging the ball through the mud, he looked up to see Ramallets off his line, and lobbed that same heavy ball precisely over the goalkeeper and under the crossbar – like a golfer, chipping out of a sand trap and landing next to the pin. It was 4-2, and for the remaining minutes England played keep-ball, the Spaniards unable to do anything about it.

1961

Another visit from north of the border now.

How Scotland and their supporters must have looked forward to this biennial visit to the old stadium. Scottish people are no more football crazy than people of other nations. It only appears that they are. Those who are old enough will remember the song Robin Hall and Jimmie MacGregor, that loveable Scottish duo, used to sing:

'For he's fitba crazy, he's fitba mad,

Fitba it has robbed him o the wee bit o sense he had.

And it would tak a dozen scivvies his clothes tae wesh and scrub,

Since our Jock became a member o that terrible fitba club.

Oh his wife she says she'll leave him, if he disna keep

Awa frae fitba kickin at night time in his sleep.

For he calls her Charlie Tully, and other names sae droll

Last night he kicked her out o bed, and shouted 'It's a GOAL!'

For he's fitba crazy...' (etc. etc.)

To 1961 then, and a day the Tartan Army will want to forget.

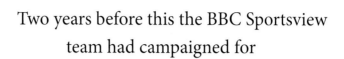

Two years before this the BBC Sportsview team had campaigned for JOHNNY HAYNES to be dropped from the England team. Haynes had responded by scoring a hat-trick against Russia. Kenneth Wolstenholme appeared before the TV cameras in sackcloth and ashes.

This was Celtic's BILLY McNEILL's first international, but not one he would remember with any pleasure.

Here he is six years later, the first British captain to lift the European Cup.

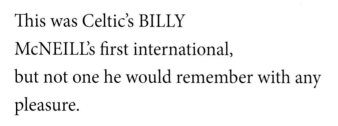

Poor Frank Haffey.

He was very well liked in Scotland, with the crowds and with the other players. No nicer person ever pulled on a goalkeeper's jersey. Haffey was a comedian and later became a pop singer.

But this was his bad hair day. He was blamed for four of the goals, and one of his colleagues thought he might have saved six of them. But he didn't deserve all of the blame. His defence gave him precious little cover – surprisingly, because Billy McNeill, Dave Mackay and Eric Caldow were great players. They simply went absent.

Bobby Robson scored first, from a distance. This was one that Haffey should have saved. Immediately his confidence evaporated, and Jimmy Greaves added two more. For the only time in the match Scotland showed some fibre, and brought the score back to 3-2.

In the second half the floodgates opened and after Bryan Douglas shot England's fourth, Bobby Smith and Johnny Haynes got a couple each and Greaves completed his hat-trick.

Mercifully England stopped at nine. Haffey left the pitch in tears at the same time as the men in white carried their captain on a lap of honour, holding the Home International Championship trophy aloft.

Haynes had played a superb game, not just scoring goals himself, but spraying defence-splitting passes for his colleagues to run on to.

Wembley clearly suited Smith. In four appearances there for club and country in 1960/61 he scored six times, all at the same end.

It all looked good for England as they prepared for another assault on the World Cup in Chile in a year's time.

1961

The Spurs team of the early 1960s did all the old-fashioned footballing things well. They trapped the ball, passed it, ran with it, ran without it, threw it in and shot it between the posts. And better and more often than all the other teams in the First Division. So when they arrived at Wembley on the first Saturday in May 1961, they had already won the championship in style and were looking to become the first team to do the 'double' in the 20th century.

From back to front they were the complete outfit, driven from midfield by skipper Danny Blanchflower and barrel-chested Scot Dave Mackay. Goals flowed from a rampant attack – 115 in the league and plenty more in the cup.

Their shrewd manager was Bill Nicholson, a former player in the famous First Division-winning 'push and run' team of the early 1950s.

So what chance had Leicester, their opponents that day at Wembley? They did have Gordon Banks, a brilliant young goalkeeper who would one day soon become England's first choice. But the Foxes would need more than that.

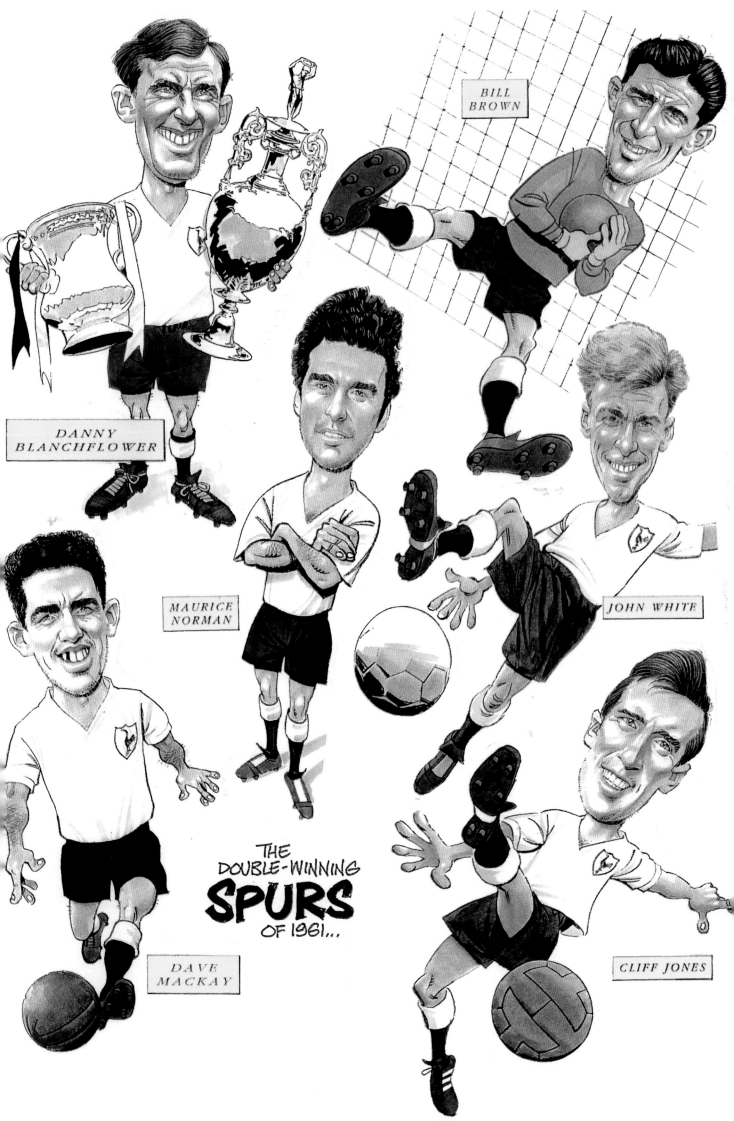

So once again the Wembley injury hoodoo took his prisoner and Leicester City, second favourites to begin with, were doomed to defeat. Spurs were not at their best. City identified Blanchflower and Mackay as the engine room, and marked them so closely that they had little space to work their usual magic. White, too, was unable to influence proceedings as he normally would. In spite of losing Chalmers, who fell in agony when trying to challenge Allen for possession, Leicester were still very much in the game when the half-time whistle blew. Their manager, Matt Gillies, then made the brave decision to, 'Go for it. We're a man down, but let's throw caution to the winds and get the winning goal.' Leicester huffed and puffed, but never really endangered Brown's goal. Young McIlmoyle was in Norman's pocket. And it was Spurs who made the breakthrough. Midway through the second half Bobby Smith dummied his marker and shot fiercely and accurately past Banks.

It was a brilliantly taken goal and fit to win any game. Dyson's header, beautifully made by Smith, simply confirmed that the cup, and the double, would be going to Spurs.

1962

Following the acquisition of Jimmy Greaves, Spurs should have been an even better team, but unaccountably lost the league championship to the unfancied tractor boys of Ipswich Town, managed by one of their old boys, Alf Ramsey.

Spurs did progress to the FA Cup Final again, so the old stadium was familiar to them. Not so to Burnley, their opponents. But the Clarets had been First Division champions two years previously, so should have posed more of a threat than Leicester did on Spurs' last visit.

After the early goal from Greaves, Spurs always looked in control, and even when Robson scored his excellent equaliser the Londoners regained the lead within a minute. They were never again in danger of not winning.

As in the previous year, Smith applied the killer punch. Socks down, he expertly controlled White's cross and fairly hammered it past Blacklaw.

The margin was still only one goal, so Burnley believed they had a chance until Blanchflower's penalty went in. Cummings had stopped Medwin's goalbound shot with his hand and suffered the consequences.*

Spurs just about deserved to keep the FA Cup for another year.

*Nowadays Cummings would have been sent to the dressing room and made to sit out the rest of the game. Surely a penalty to the opposition is sufficient punishment?

1962

1965

Alf Ramsey had taken over as England's manager after Walter Winterbottom's long period in charge came to an end in 1962.

Walter's last appearance was at Wembley, appropriately, but it was watched by the lowest ever crowd at an international match at the stadium. England beat Wales comfortably and Jimmy Greaves scored the last goal of Walter's reign.

Ramsey didn't have an auspicious start – a 5-2 defeat to France in Paris – but there was never any doubt that he would be in charge when England hosted the World Cup in 1966. Already Alf was promising that England would win it, although he had only three truly world-class players at his disposal. The rest were good, professional, hard-working men who wouldn't let him down.

When Scotland visited Wembley in 1965 Ramsey gave debuts to Nobby Stiles and to Jack Charlton. England's defence that day was man for man the same as would play in the World Cup. Some of the attacking positions were still up for grabs. Barry Bridges, Johnny Byrne and Peter Thompson were tried in this game.

DENIS LAW enjoyed Wembley's wide-open spaces. He scored the opening goal when Manchester United beat Leicester in the 1963 FA Cup Final, and was prominent in some happy Scottish wins over the Old Enemy, again in 1963 and also in 1967.

On his two visits to Wembley in 1965 IAN ST. JOHN was a goalscorer on both occasions, not only in this international, but also in the FA Cup Final when he was in the right place at the right time.

ENGLAND 2 SCOTLAND 2

BILL BROWN IN SCOTLAND'S GOAL SPORTED A SILLY BASEBALL CAP,

WHICH IS PROBABLY WHY HE DIDN'T SAVE BOBBY CHARLTON'S OPENER.

OTHER FRIENDSHIPS WERE ALSO STRAINED AS MEN FROM THE SAME CLUBS CLASHED.

STILES, ON HIS ENGLAND DEBUT, RAN ALL OVER HIS UNITED COLLEAGUE CRERAND.

IN THE CONTEST TO SEE WHOSE FACE WOULD ATTRACT THE LADIES, BRIDGES BEAT McCREADIE EASILY...

ENGLAND MIGHT HAVE WON IF THE WEMBLEY INJURY HOODOO HAD NOT MADE AN UNTIMELY APPEARANCE.

SO THEY PLAYED THE SECOND HALF WITH ONLY NINE AND A HALF FIT MEN.

OH STINK...

HAVE WE KICKED OFF, THEN?

HE'D HAVE HAD A BETTER CHANCE OF SAVING IT IF HE'D THROWN HIS RIDICULOUS HAT AT THE BALL... GREAVES MADE IT 2-0 WITH A GOAL WHICH WAS PURE TEXTILE.

HE HAD NO SECOND THOUGHTS ABOUT WHIZZING ONE PAST HIS SPURS TEAM MATE.

PICK THAT ONE OUT, BILL!

THAT'S JUST TO REMIND YOU I'M HERE, PADDY...

YOU'LL NEED A STEPLADDER, WEE FELLA...

JACK CHARLTON, IN ANOTHER FIRST APPEARANCE, OUTJUMPED HIS LEEDS MATE COLLINS,

AND THOMPSON COULD ONLY WATCH FROM A DISTANCE AS HIS KOP BUDDY ST JOHN EQUALISED FOR SCOTLAND

NOW LET'S SEE... WHO SHALL I NOBBLE THIS TIME?

THAT'S SCREWED UP MY DAY...

BOBBY MOORE, ALL ELEGANCE AND STYLE, SO WITH THE AFORE-MENTIONED JACK AND NOBBY, THIS IS THE HALF-BACK LINE WHICH ALF THINKS WILL BE IN PLACE FOR NEXT YEAR'S WORLD CUP.

Bob Bond

An incident-packed match at Wembley saw England do well to come away with a draw after a spirited rearguard action when they lost two of their players to injuries.

The game began in torrential rain, and there were puddles on the pitch at the kick-off. Then out came the sun and conditions improved. Bobby Charlton gave England the lead with a swerving shot which Brown should have saved. Charlton then sent Greaves galloping through to shoot the second, and England were well worth their comfortable lead.

Brown was not the only goalkeeper at fault, as Banks made of hash at saving a shot from Law and it was 2-1 at the interval. England's Wilson had already been injured, and early in the second half Byrne was seen to be hobbling and he was reduced to being simply a passenger on the left wing.

What an opportunity for Scotland, but it was then that the Englishmen defended heroically, with Bobby Charlton in a strange position at full-back.

But he played superbly, as did his brother Jack on his debut. Moore, too, was faultless. Scotland did scramble an equaliser, but that was all they got. Every one of the remaining England players ran themselves into the ground. But the Scots would be disappointed that they couldn't turn their numerical advantage into a victory.

1965

In 1965 Liverpool and Leeds United were still both a work in progress, and greater years lay ahead for them. Liverpool, with their astute manager Bill Shankly, had spent three years back in the top flight. Shankly's was much the same settled team that had won promotion from the Second Division in 1962 and had won the First Division title in 1964.

Leeds, too, had a knowledgeable manager in place. Don Revie had brought them out of the second tier in 1964 and they had made an immediate impact on the top flight as they finished second behind Manchester United only with an inferior goal average. The teams lined up at Wembley for the red rose against the white, red shirts and shorts against all white.

Shankly and Revie knew what it was like to win here as players. Liverpool would be without the injured Gordon Milne whose father Jimmy had coincidentally missed the 1938 final for the same reason.

A clever wee inside-forward, BOBBY COLLINS was coming towards the end of a long and distinguished career with Celtic, Everton and Leeds when he made his final Wembley appearance in this game.

IAN CALLAGHAN had barely started his tenure at Liverpool. This was the first time he ran out on to the Wembley pitch, but not the last. He played here a few more times for Liverpool, and had one game for England in the 1966 World Cup.

It was very much as the experts predicted, with Liverpool slightly more adventurous, with a bit more flair; Leeds were dour, rather more defensive, relying on the occasional breakaway, but still a hard nut to crack. And it rained.

In the third minute Bobby Collins clashed over-zealously with Gerry Byrne, and got rather a stern lecture from the referee. Byrne didn't get off so lightly, and emerged from the challenge with what he later found out was a broken collar bone. He refused to leave the action. He didn't expect extra time as well, but

that's where the game went, with still no goals. If you were measuring figures like possession, zonal action, and shots at goal, as the statisticians do nowadays, Liverpool would have had the edge. But they had barely looked like breaking the deadlock.

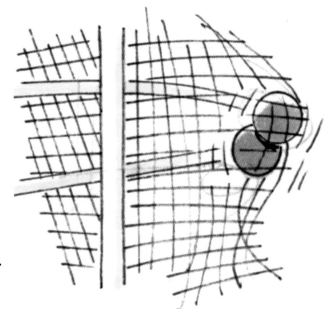

Soon after extra time began, Liverpool scored, when Byrne, still battling on bravely, crossed for Roger Hunt to head in. The Leeds equaliser was as good as it was unexpected. Charlton headed the ball down and Bremner struck it first time, on the half-volley. Lawrence didn't move until he picked the ball out of his net. But St John then met Callaghan's centre for the winner.

'The Leeds goal looked as big as the Mersey Tunnel, so I just headed it in,' he said. Liverpool just deserved to win.

Wembley was kind to West Ham United in the mid-1960s. RON BOYCE headed the winning goal when they carried off the FA Cup in 1964, and they followed this with the European Cup Winners' Cup a year later. Boyce, pictured here, had another splendid game against 1860 Munich.

It was his precise pass that Sealey seized on before firing the Hammers ahead midway through the second half, and before the Germans could recover, the same player popped in a second.

But it was not a one-man victory. From back to front, West Ham were excellent.

Moore was immaculate and Sissons, who twice hit the woodwork, was a constant danger. Here is centre-half KEN BROWN, commanding as ever in defence and ready to die for the cause.

Not many years later they went on to win the FA Cup twice more, and in one of those finals Bobby Moore, nearing the end of his career, lined up for Fulham against West Ham.

1966

As the new year dawned Everton were in a perilous position in the First Division. Relegation, that dirty word, was being spoken of as the Toffees plunged down the table. To make matters worse for their followers, Liverpool were top.

For a visit to Blackpool in January, boss Harry Catterick dropped Alex Young and replaced him with teenager Joe Royle. Joe had a decent game, but Everton lost again. One supporter was so irate that, after the match, he took a flying kick at Mr Catterick. It was the only Everton shot that found the target that day. In your wildest dreams you would never have imagined Everton winning anything that season.

Young, the fans' favourite, was restored to the team, who then set off on a run of victories which secured their league safety and took them right through to the FA Cup Final.

Everton's opponents were Sheffield Wednesday. Yes, it is a strange name for a football club. In the USA, someone on a sports desk wrote an article about an American player going to Sheffield Wednesday, and a football-ignorant editor changed it to, 'John Harkes going to Sheffield on Wednesday.'

Neither Wednesday nor Everton had been at Wembley since before the war. Harry Catterick made another brave selection, leaving out leading scorer Fred Pickering and replacing him with Mike Trebilcock, a comparatively unknown Cornishman.

As she met the teams, Princess Margaret asked BRIAN LABONE 'Where exactly IS Everton?'

'We are from Liverpool,' Labone replied.

So she said, 'Ah yes – we had your first team here last year.'

Despite being a loser this time, JIM McCALLIOG would have some better days at Wembley.

He scored in Scotland's defeat of England in 1967, then got his cup winner's medal with Southampton in 1976.

So Catterick's decision to play Trebilcock instead of Pickering paid off, big time. Everton just about deserved to win, but Wednesday played their part in making this a very watchable final.

When young Jim McCalliog gave them an early lead, they forced Everton to come out to play. Wednesday held on, in spite of a good claim for a penalty and a disallowed goal for offside that wasn't, and then they increased their advantage early in the second half. All chewed up for the Toffees? Not likely. Enter the Cornishman with two opportunist goals, one to Springett's right and one to his left. It was all up for grabs now, as one well-known commentator would one day famously say, and as Wednesday's Young faltered, Temple ran on to win the cup. Once again Springett's dive just couldn't reach the ball.

Usually the losers troop away, leaving the stage to the victors, but Wednesday's skipper Megson insisted his team did a lap of honour after the match. They had certainly played their part in making this an end-to-end, entertaining final.

And yes, one over-enthusiastic Everton supporter left his trousers out on the Wembley pitch. Was he the same man who had kicked Catterick at Blackpool not so long ago?

1966

Those of us who were alive all know where we were, don't we, on the day England won the World Cup, Saturday, 30 July 1966.

The lucky 100,000 were at Wembley, inside the stadium. But millions more of us were watching on television, and hearing Kenneth Wolstenholme's immortal words, 'Some people are on the pitch. They think it's all over. It is, now.'

So a few of us were actually on the pitch that day. Some of us were playing our own sport. Playing cricket, would you believe? Why, oh why, wasn't all the cricket cancelled that day? We may have been on the pitch, yes, but totally the wrong pitch. The other team, calling out the score, the goals as they were going in, news from a distant pavilion. We recall that feeling of deflation when West Germany equalised, then the opposite feeling of elation at Geoff Hurst's extra-time goals. England had won it, proving once again that at football we were still the best in the world. For the time being, anyway.

Yes, if we were alive in 1966, we know where we were.

But how did England arrange to play all their games at Wembley? Never mind, they just did.

ENGLAND 2 FRANCE 0

THE FRENCH MAY WIN THE TOUR DE FRANCE AGAIN THIS YEAR. BUT AT SOCCER RIGHT NOW THEY ARE A PETIT PUSHOVER.

CATCH ME EEF YOU CAN...

SNAIL EATING CONTEST

ENGLAND DID NOT NEED TO BE AT THEIR BEST TO ENSURE THAT OUR SNAIL-MUNCHING NEIGHBOURS GO BACK ACROSS THE CHANNEL WITH NO MORE INTEREST IN THIS TOURNAMENT.

THAT WELL-KNOWN SCOUSER ROGER HUNT SOCKED IT TO THEM WITH A GOAL IN EACH HALF. TO WHICH THE GALLIC ONZE COULD NOT REPLY.

DIDN'T I DO WELL? KISS ME ONE MORE TIME...

THEY PROTESTED TO THE REFEREE THAT ONE OF THE DODGER'S GOALS WAS OFFSIDE...

GO AWAY MON AMI... OR I SHALL BOOK YOU FOR HAVING GARLIC BREATH...

SIMON WAS THE ONLY FRENCH PLAYER TO THREATEN, BUT AT TIMES HE HAD TO WAIT FOR HIS BRAIN TO CATCH UP WITH HIS LEGS. STILES TOOK CARE OF SIMON ANYWAY.

SO... NOW BRING ON GARFUNKEL...

THE FRENCH, WHO NEEDED TWO MORE GOALS THAN ENGLAND, WERE SHOT-SHY. THEY FINISHED WITH NIL, WHICH WAS ABOUT WHAT THEY MERITED

OOOH... SOME POSTS AND AN ONION BAG. WHAT DO I DO NOW?

GORDON BANKS IS STILL TO CONCEDE A GOAL. HE DID WHAT HE HAD TO DO FLAWLESSLY.

PICK THAT ONE OUT, HANS...

1·0 TO GERMANY, THEN, ENGLAND HAD TO WIN, NOT ONLY BECAUSE THEY ARE ENGLISH, BUT BECAUSE THE PARTY WAS AT THEIR HOUSE.

SO, QUITE RIGHTLY AND PROPERLY, THEY TURNED IT AROUND. HURST, 1-1...

A FREE-KICK FROM WHICH WEST GERMANY SCORED. 2-2, AND EXTRA-TIME.

WELL... THAT'S A PROPER PARTY POOPER...

SKIPPER BOBBY MOORE WITH HIS HANDS ON THE TROPHY

ALF COULD AFFORD TO SMILE AT LAST.

WHAT DID I SAY ALL ALONG?

FOR JIMMY GREAVES THERE WILL BE MIXED FEELINGS RIGHT NOW...

FUNNY OLD GAME...

NEVER MIND, DEAR, THEY WON WITHOUT YOU...

THIS SHOULD HAVE BEEN **HIS** DAY.

England v Uruguay

'The expectancy at the kick-off was soon gone, as the Uruguayans negatively began their campaign. True, they had some skilful players and Rocha, Viera and Silva all showed glimpses of their abilities. A fierce shot from Cortes forced Banks into a save early on, but that proved a rare moment of adventure for the South Americans. In the last minute Connelly back-heeled the ball inches wide. The evening ended in total frustration.'

England v Mexico

'Peters intercepted a Mexican pass and moved the ball on to Hunt. His quick pass sent Bobby Charlton on his way, from just inside his own half. With his thinning hair streaming in the wind, he continued at pace, then from 25 yards out his right boot sent a blockbuster into the top corner of Calderon's net. It was vintage Charlton.'

England v France

'Stiles clearly fouled Simon with a late and unsavoury tackle. The Peruvian referee ignored it, allowing Callaghan to cross perfectly for his Liverpool team-mate Hunt to head his second goal of the night. The tackle was questionable enough for some important FA members to wonder if Stiles should still be in Ramsey's team.'

England v Argentina

'As tempers rose, the referee struggled to keep a grip on proceedings and his pencil began working overtime. Rattin, Artime and Solari were all booked, and with ten minutes of the first half remaining, all hell broke loose. With the ball elsewhere, Mr Kreitlein was seen to be pointing towards the dressing room, having sent Rattin off. Bedlam ensued. Players and officials jostled on the pitch, and at one point it seemed like the whole Argentine team would walk off. Eventually order was restored and the game continued.'

England v Portugal

'Full-back Cohen sent a long ball forward for Hurst to chase. He cleverly gained possession and waited for support to arrive – and did not have to wait long – here came Bobby Charlton, storming through. Hurst laid the ball back perfectly into his path and wham! It flew past Pereira and, leaping with pleasure, all the England players ran to Charlton to celebrate.'

England v West Germany

'Ball collected the pass from Stiles and centred instantly. Hurst trapped the ball and, with his back to goal, swivelled and crashed in a tremendous shot which thudded against the crossbar, bounced down and was hurriedly cleared by a German defender. "Goal!" shouted the England players. The Germans disagreed, claiming the ball had not crossed the line. The referee ran over to his Russian linesman, and after a tense conversation and an agonising wait Mr Dienst pointed to the middle. 3-2, and England could once again celebrate. The Germans were far from happy.'

GEOFF HURST began the World Cup as a reserve, but ended it as the nation's hero.

Neither was ALAN BALL a first choice when the tournament began. But his non-stop running was a feature of the later rounds.

Fulham's full-back GEORGE COHEN was another player who got better and better as the weeks went by.

And here is
PICKLES
the dog,
who
when we
carelessly
lost the trophy, found it so
that England could win
it and keep it safe for the
next four years.

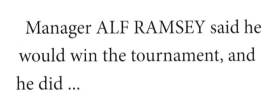

Manager ALF RAMSEY said he would win the tournament, and he did ...

November 1966

As the year drew to a close the whole country was still basking in World Cup glory. Not surprisingly Bobby Moore won the BBC Sports Personality of the Year award, and England's footballers Team of the Year. We awoke every morning pinching ourselves.

'Did England really do it? Is that Jules Rimet Trophy still in our cabinet?'

Man for man, England wheeled out the same team for a Home International match in Belfast and beat Northern Ireland comfortably.

Then, in November, they returned to Wembley, the scene of their wonderful triumph a few months earlier.

If the crowd expected a party, Czechoslovakia came only to poop it, and with a nine-man defensive wall, they smothered every England move. Nil-nil at full time, that had been the score at half-time as well.

Two weeks later Wales arrived at Wembley for another Home International, which also doubled as a European qualifier.

Wales, surely, would be a bit more adventurous?

RON DAVIES plundered plenty of goals for Norwich, Southampton and Wales.

RAY WILSON, another of England's World Cup men, kept his full-back place for a few more years. He was also an FA Cup winner with Everton in 1966.

England were flattered by the final scoreline, which in no way reflected the way the game went.

It was a bitterly cold evening, but 76,000 brave spectators enjoyed an end-to-end scrap. At first England missed some good opportunities, Hurst being the main culprit. The West Ham man persevered and eventually one of his shots sailed past Millington to put England ahead. Stiles then crossed perfectly for Hurst to head a beauty. Who said Nobby lacked finesse?

Moments later Wales shocked England by pulling a goal back, Wyn Davies heading past Banks. But before half-time Bobby Charlton restored the two goal advantage with a shot Millington should have saved. Charlton didn't care – he now had 41 goals for his country.

Bobby Moore, on his 50th international appearance, was as commanding as ever.

The decisive moment came early in the second half when Ron Davies smacked a shot against a post. A goal then would have lifted Wales, but England went on to increase their lead when first Terry Hennessey put through his own goal, and then Jack Charlton headed a fifth.

'Tiny' Wharton, the Scottish referee, ruled over the proceedings firmly. But who would ever argue with such a massive presence?

The result seemed totally unfair to Wales, who had fought so hard.

1967

Scotland must have been preparing for this day for a long time. Their team and their supporters were ready to knock England off their lofty pedestal. It wasn't envy, but just a fierce determination to prove something. If you were in London that weekend, you could feel it, and almost touch it. The old rivalry was bubbling.

At the same time Celtic were preparing for a different assault, on the European Cup. They already had one foot in the final, having beaten Dukla Prague in the first leg of their semi. And four of their brilliant team would be on view at Wembley, including their 37-year-old goalkeeper Ron Simpson. He had good Wembley memories – two FA Cup winner's medals gained with Newcastle years previously.

At the other end of the age scale was 20-year-old Jim McCalliog of Sheffield Wednesday.

Pencil-slim JIM BAXTER had also inspired a Scottish victory at Wembley in 1963. He was not quite so slim when he headed south to play for Sunderland and Forest.

What a year 1967 was for BOBBY LENNOX! A scorer at Wembley, and a European Cup winner with Celtic.

And for RON SIMPSON. Remember him? Goalkeeper in two of Newcastle's FA Cup winning sides in the 1950s, and here he was, 12 years later, still stopping the shots.

If England began as favourites, they trudged off disappointed at losing their long unbeaten record. It had been 19 matches since they last had their colours lowered.

The highlight for any Scottish team is a victory over the Auld Enemy, but to do it over the world champions gave them extra satisfaction.

Understandably they now claimed that they, and not England, were champions of the world!

England had to contend with a few knocks as the cartoon shows. Big Jack Charlton broke a toe when tackling Lennox, and the returning Jimmy Greaves also limped away with a swollen ankle after a challenge.

When Ray Wilson was reduced to half-pace England had only eight fit men. This mustn't detract from Scotland's achievement. They took the game by the scruff of the neck from the kick-off and Law, with typical sharpness, fired past Banks to put them one up. Wembley was a sea of tartan hats and scarves.

That looked like it would be enough, as the Scots seemed content with a one-goal victory, but in the last ten minutes there was a goal rush.

Two of the Celtic men combined when Lennox scored from a long pass by Gemmell. Then the limping Jack Charlton poked the ball into Scotland's net following a goalmouth scramble. McCalliog, the baby of the team, restored the two-goal advantage before Hurst headed England's second. There was barely time to restart before the German referee blew for the end of the game and the start of the Tartan Army's celebrations.

1968

Wednesday, 29 May 1968, and Wembley stadium had been allocated the final of the European Cup. All it needed was for an English team to be involved.

For a decade and more, Manchester United manager Matt Busby had dreamed of winning this, the ultimate club competition. United were again the country's representatives – and had come through an amazing semi-final, beating the many-times-winners Real Madrid.

Such a victory had seemed impossible when United trailed at half-time in the second leg in Madrid. They had been steamrollered into the ground by a superb Real.

But amazingly United rose again and scored two goals without reply, the last one turned in to the net by an unlikely marksman – skipper Bill Foulkes.

So with Wembley stadium looking its very best, expectant fans from Manchester and from Lisbon filed in.

Bring it on!

There was nobody quite like GEORGE BEST, and here he was teasing Benfica, just as he had done in Lisbon two years previously.

FOULKES was back at Wembley again after helping United win the FA Cup here in 1963.

EUSEBIO, a brilliant player, but twice a loser at Wembley, once for Benfica, then Portugal. Would this be third time unlucky?

It was a very warm evening at Wembley when two of Europe's most famous sides confronted each other in the final of the European Cup.

Celtic had taken the trophy back to Scotland the previous year, so what could England's best do?

Eusebio, who had starred at Wembley for Portugal in the World Cup, again lit up the stadium with his brilliance. His sudden shot bounced back off the crossbar. Shocked into action, United should have taken the lead themselves, but Sadler shot wide with only Henrique to beat.

Soon after half-time Sadler made amends, crossing for Bobby Charlton to score with a glancing header. At 1-0 United were never comfortable, and such was Benfica's brilliance that an equaliser was always on.

It came ten minutes from the end, Graca beating Stepney with a low shot from a Torres pass. Benfica's chance to win it fell to Eusebio, but this time Stepney saved brilliantly.

In extra time, blue-shirted United took control. Goalkeeper Stepney's long clearance was headed on by Kidd to Best, who rounded Henrique and slid the ball into the net. Henrique was soon picking another one out, a header from Kidd this time. And then Charlton turned in Kidd's centre for a third goal in six wonderful minutes!

'This is my greatest moment,' said Matt Busby. 'I have planned this for a long time. I am a happy man tonight.'

1969

It was a tale of two cities again at Wembley, as Manchester City, having beatend Birmingham City in the 1956 final, did the same to Leicester City.

The deciding goal was set up by MIKE SUMMERBEE and finished emphatically by NEIL YOUNG.

Wembley was once again unkind to the Foxes who had now been to the FA Cup Final FOUR times since the war and not won any of them. Their fans must have been fed up with this repeat prescription.

Young Peter Shilton had replaced Gordon Banks between the sticks and was predicted to do just as well. He had no chance with the goal.

TONY BOOK, plucked from obscurity by Malcolm Allison, received the trophy from Princess Anne.

The referee used a new seven-sided 50 pence coin for the toss-up. Ones like it would soon be in circulation. But not the one he used. For the losers Allan Clarke had a fine game, and was destined for great things.

1970

And here was the same ALLAN CLARKE, now a Leeds United player, back at Wembley the following year. But that pitch was not worthy of Wembley. It was worse than a ploughed field. Nevertheless, Leeds were brilliant, and clearly the better team.

EDDIE GRAY led David Webb a merry dance. But Chelsea simply refused to be beaten. Their first goal was a mistake by Sprake, who let a simple shot slip through his careless hands.

Their second equaliser was a fine header by Ian Hutchinson just as Leeds relaxed their guard, thinking the game was won.

PETER BONETTI was superb in Chelsea's goal, and CHARLIE COOKE showed flashes of magic.

After extra time it was still level. All those Wembley finals, and this was the first one to end in a draw. Although Leeds had been the favourites, the replay was deservedly won by Chelsea.

We promised no statistics, but here is one worth breaking that promise with. It took Stoke City more than 100 years to win their first major trophy. They had never been to Wembley before, but in 1972 they beat Chelsea to win the League Cup Final.

Their shrewd manager TONY WADDINGTON was known for signing experienced players, who other clubs had cast off, reckoning them over the hill.

GORDON BANKS was back at Wembley picking up another trophy. And more was to follow as he was named FWA Footballer of the Year.

This is flame-haired TERRY CONROY, who scored Stoke's first goal at Wembley.

Chelsea had a good team, and were ten places higher than Stoke in the First Division table. Far left is PETER OSGOOD who equalised.

And RON HARRIS, rightly nicknamed 'Chopper', because that's what he did.

But he arrived too late to stop GEORGE EASTHAM from poking in Stoke's winner. Eastham, the Peter Pan of football, had last played at Wembley for England many years earlier.

And here's another oldie, PETER DOBING, City's captain, with the trophy.

1973

Unless our own club was involved and we were lucky enough to get a ticket, most of us watched the cup finals on television.

And as a Leeds United defender smashed into a Sunderland man sideways, hard enough to send him spinning out of his shorts, a restrained David Coleman would say, 'An interesting challenge, that, by Madeley.'

Leeds were a hard team in every sense of the word. Having won the centenary FA Cup Final in 1972, they returned to Wembley the following year with every likelihood of retaining the trophy. In the late 1960s and early 1970s they were the most powerful side in England, and with a bit more of a smile from Dame Fortune would have collected more honours than they did. Leeds finished in the top three of the First Division for six consecutive years, and every player in the team had played for his country.

What a contrast were their opponents at Wembley that afternoon, as Sunderland were from the Second Division – a team of hard triers but no-hopers, really. At one time in the season they had been in danger of dropping into the third tier. Unlike Leeds, none of their players were household names, although Dennis Tueart later found greater fame with Manchester City and England, and Dave Watson would go on to win plenty of international caps.

Bob Stokoe, a Wembley winner with Newcastle as a player, was their likeable manager.

This wasn't the last medal DENNIS TUEART won at Wembley. On another occasion, for Manchester City, he chose a League Cup Final to show the world his beautiful bicycle kick.

Scottish winger PETER LORIMER was reputed to have the hardest shot in football at this time. You wouldn't want to be in its path. But on this day Montgomery denied him.

David beating Goliath is one of the most endearing stories, and close to all our hearts. Defying all the odds, Sunderland were worthy winners. None of their players shirked a tackle or gave less than 100 per cent. Red and white stripes were everywhere.

Every man ran and ran until his legs were ready to fall off. Their powers of recovery were remarkable. Olga Korbut would have been impressed with Jim Montgomery's double save from Cherry and Lorimer which defied all acrobatic reason.

Eddie Gray, the player who owned Wembley in the final three years earlier, was in Malone's pocket. He was so powerless that Don Revie was forced to take him off and send on substitute Yorath. But to no avail. Gray was not alone. All over the field Leeds were outfought and outjumped. Was there a better centre-half in England than Watson? Once a centre-forward, he was now a rock in defence.

As the cartoon shows, Porterfield volleyed the only goal of the game after a corner kick by Hughes had created panic in the Leeds goalmouth.

At the final whistle Stokoe also ran and ran, until he had hugged every one of his brave battlers. And there was a special hug for Monty.

October 1973

England had got themselves into a bit of a mess, seeking to qualify for the next World Cup finals in West Germany. They had to beat Poland at Wembley. If they didn't, perish the thought, Poland would go instead.

It should not have come down to the wire like this. Everything would be okay, of course, as Alf's men had warmed up with a hearty 7-0 thumping of Austria in a friendly at Wembley a fortnight earlier.

The Austrian defence had been helpless against England's Clarke, Channon, Chivers and Currie – and at the end they were on their knees.

'England can still teach the world how to play this game,' admitted the Austrian manager as he left Wembley with his bedraggled team.

More of the same, then. Poland were better than Austria, but not much better. And their goalkeeper was a weak link that England would exploit, as television pundit Brian Clough famously predicted.

Here is NORMAN HUNTER, a terrific wing-half for Leeds and for England. But this would not be one of his favourite Wembley memories.

MARTIN CHIVERS was a strong centre-forward, first with Southampton, then Spurs and England. He scored twice for Tottenham at Wembley in a League Cup Final victory over Aston Villa.

So Alf's men didn't win, and so could only watch the World Cup finals in West Germany. Poland went instead of England*.

Tomaszewski was the star performer on the night although, as the cartoon shows, some of his saves were eccentric in the extreme. England totalled 35 goal attempts in the 90 minutes, and yet scored just once from the penalty spot. Poland had only two shots at goal, Domarski converting one of them following Hunter's defensive slip. Even then, Shilton would have saved the shot most days of the week.

Ramsey sent on Kevin Hector near the end, and the Derby County man headed England's last opportunity inches wide. Had this gone in, it might have changed the course of English football. They would have gone to those finals and maybe won the World Cup once more, and Alf's job would have been secured.

The old stadium must have looked on the proceedings with sorrow. It was one of Wembley's most frustrating evenings and signalled the end of Ramsey's reign as manager. Within a few months he was gone.

* Poland did well, finishing in third place behind West Germany and Holland.

1974

This would be Shankly's parting reminder to his boys on the Friday before the big game.

He need not have worried about the chastity of his players as they prepared to meet Newcastle United in the FA Cup Final.

OCH— SLEEP IN YOUR OWN BED TONIGHT...

Newcastle were expected to be strong opposition, with Malcolm Macdonald at his bulldozing best. But it didn't happen. The match was one-sided. The only surprise was the length of time it took for Liverpool to open their account. A whole hour elapsed before KEVIN KEEGAN did the business.

The Liverpool fans called STEVE HEIGHWAY 'Big Bamber' and BRIAN HALL 'Little Bamber' because of their university education – a sly reference to Bamber Gascoigne, the original host of University Challenge.

They also had a nickname for EMLYN HUGHES. He was 'Crazy Horse', because that's what he was. A great player, and a captain on *A Question of Sport*, Emlyn died far too young.

Heighway scored the second, and then Keegan gave the scoreline a realistic appearance at a comprehensive 3-0.

BOBBY MONCUR did his best to stem the tide.

TERRY McDERMOTT and ALAN KENNEDY were losers that day at Wembley. But winners later on as both joined Liverpool, and both scored vital goals in European Cup Finals.

Traditionally the Charity Shield match between the league champions and the FA Cup winners is a curtain-raiser for every season, played one week before the new campaign begins in earnest. It is a coveted trophy, hard fought for, but the game is not usually over-aggressive as players don't want to risk injury before the real business begins.

In 1974 the Charity Shield was contested for at Wembley for the first time, and was clearly expected to be a relatively friendly showpiece between two of the country's best teams.

But those teams were Liverpool and Leeds United, and there was history and fierce rivalry between the two. Bill Shankly had announced his retirement. After years of success, with FA Cup wins and league championships, he was stepping down. He led out Liverpool for the last time, enthusiastically greeted by the fans and applauded all the way to the middle by the Leeds United manager. That man was leading out his team for the first time. His name was Brian Clough.

The 1972 FA Cup Final was the centenary one, and was won by Leeds. Clarke headed the winning goal which was set up by MICK JONES. It was a bitter-sweet game for Jones, who later fell and dislocated a collarbone. His painful climb to receive his medal was excruciating to watch.

Welsh striker JOHN TOSHACK was the other half of Liverpool's wonderful 'smash and grab' double act with Kevin Keegan.

'Wembley's Day of Shame' was the headline in one newspaper the following day. So it was not the spectacle that had been hoped for.

Matches between Liverpool and Leeds have always been quite physical encounters, but never have they erupted into all-out war.

It began early on, as Allan Clarke's late tackle took the skin off Phil Thompson's shin. Referee Bob Matthewson thought little of it, but Liverpool were steaming. A few minutes later Tommy Smith took revenge, upending Clarke right in front of the official, who promptly booked Smith.

The roughness continued and was clearly going to bubble right over before the game ended. Keegan and Giles had been niggling at each other for a while, before suddenly Giles swung a punch at his opponent. Into the referee's book went Johnny.

Matthewson didn't want to be the first ref to send off a player from a British team at Wembley. But when Keegan and Bremner began exchanging punches, he was left with no other course of action.

As they walked off the field both men tore off their shirts and left them for someone else to pick up. They kept their shorts on, thankfully. Both faced a hefty fine and a lengthy ban. The result of the match didn't seem to matter.

1975

Joe Mercer had taken over from Alf Ramsey as England's manager in 1974, but it was always going to be a temporary appointment until the right man became available.

The right man appeared to be Don Revie, who'd had considerable success as a manager at club level. Like Mercer, he had good and less good memories of Wembley. He had a cup winner's medal from his playing days with Manchester City, and as boss of Leeds United in the centenary FA Cup Final in 1972.

Managing a club is so different to managing a country, as Revie was to discover. He long-listed more than 80 players as England possibles, and invited them all to a meeting where he delivered a Churchillian speech, promising success on a major scale. One player refused Don's invitation. 'I'm Scottish,' said Nottingham Forest's John Robertson.

Revie also introduced a new fashion in England's football shirts, sponsored by Admiral, and asked the crowd to sing 'Land of Hope and Glory'. No controversy there, then.

But as yet, no black or coloured players were in contention for England places.

Cyprus came to stretch their legs at Wembley in April 1975 for a European Championship qualifier.

Manchester City's COLIN BELL gave many polished performances for England, and Wembley invariably brought the best out of him. In Don Revie's first game in charge of England in 1974 Bell scored two sensational goals against Czechoslovakia.

It could be argued that PETER SHILTON was England's best-ever goalkeeper, and he loved the Wembley stage. As well as representing his country more times than anyone else he also helped Nottingham Forest to two League Cup wins there.

It turned out, as you can see, to be an evening to remember for Malcolm Macdonald, as England cruised to an easy victory to stay on top of their qualifying group.

It was all England on the night as Cyprus posed little threat to Shilton's goal. After only two minutes Hudson's free kick was headed powerfully past Alkiviadis by Macdonald, and it was a lead England were never in danger of losing. They mounted wave after wave of attacks, but were too predictable and time and again a massed defence scrambled the ball away. It was last-ditch defending, and it took England half an hour to add to their lead with a thumping left-footer by Macdonald. The Cypriot goalkeeper continued to make some unbelievable saves, and some that he knew nothing about.

SuperMac's head seemed to be the simplest way to goal for England and another header early in the second half brought him to his hat-trick, to the delight of all his fans from Newcastle.

The goalkeeper was injured trying to stop Beattie from adding to the score, and Cyprus had to bring on a replacement.

England also used a substitute – Dave Thomas for Channon – and he proceeded to set up two more goals for Macdonald, both headers, of course. So he joined a select band of players who have scored five goals in one match for England, and became the first to do this at Wembley.

Kevin Keegan was the first superstar to be brought into the England team in the 1970s. Since Moore and Charlton, the country had been crying out for a player of skill and charisma, and Alf Ramsey had cautiously given Keegan his introduction to international football in 1972.

His first Wembley appearance had been against Wales a year later, where he watched his Liverpool mate Toshack score for the opposition in a 1-1 draw.

Keegan returned to the stadium a few months later. It was a much happier occasion when his two goals for Liverpool inspired them to a win over Newcastle in a one-sided FA Cup Final.

His was the first name on the team sheet when Don Revie became England's manager.

Soon after the demolition of Cyprus England welcomed the Auld Enemy back to Wembley. And there was no Malcolm Macdonald in their line up, so Scotland had every reason to believe that they could upset the England applecart.

Wembley stadium was like a home ground for goalkeeper RAY CLEMENCE. Many times he trotted up those steps and came down with a winner's medal.

DANNY McGRAIN was a classy defender for Celtic and for Scotland. When Danny tackled you, you knew you had been clobbered.

On paper, Scotland looked as good as England. Young Kenny Dalglish, destined to succeed Keegan at Liverpool, was making his second appearance for his country at Wembley. His first visit in 1973 had ended in defeat, but not as bad as this one. Bruce Rioch, Sandy Jardine and Alfie Conn were all skilful players, and Ted MacDougall had once scored nine goals in an FA Cup tie for Bournemouth.

One strike here would have boosted Scotland's chances considerably, but SuperTed was never allowed near England's goal. Scotland never recovered from the disastrous start they made, going two down in the first seven minutes.

Goalkeeper Kennedy appeared to be at fault with both goals, by Gerry Francis and Kevin Beattie. Colin Bell made it 3-0, and the Scottish threat was as good as snuffed out, even though the German referee kindly awarded them a penalty on the stroke of half-time. Rioch scored, but early in the second period Kennedy was again beaten by Francis from long range.

His confidence completely evaporated, and this seemed to affect the whole team. Johnson added a fifth, whereupon England declared their innings closed, and Scotland left the field demoralised and dispirited. Although he didn't himself score, Keegan was undoubtedly the star, throwing the Scottish defence into panic every time he got the ball.

1976

This was another surprise result, the kind that Wembley occasionally threw up in the 1970s. Manchester United were back near the top of the First Division after a sojourn in the Second Division.

They had ALEX STEPNEY, a goalkeeper from the very top bracket, and MARTIN BUCHAN, a classy Scottish defender.

Two smashing goals from GORDON HILL had sunk Derby County in the semi-final.

Southampton were from the Second Division, and most
pundits thought they were just going along to Wembley
for the ride. Peter Osgood and Jim McCalliog had played at
Wembley in previous finals for other teams, as had Peter
Rodrigues, their captain.

MICK CHANNON was another
with Wembley experience playing
for England.

But it was the unsung BOBBY STOKES
who popped up with the winner just before
the end.

'He should be given the freedom of
Hampshire,' said LAWRIE McMENEMY,
their very happy manager.

Here's PETER RODRIGUES with the trophy.

Like Sunderland and Southampton, Bobby Robson's Ipswich Town were not expected to win the FA Cup Final in 1978.

Wembley was ready for an Arsenal win. Goalkeeper PAT JENNINGS was back in the stadium where he had earlier helped Spurs to win the FA Cup in 1967.

Arsenal mistakenly gambled on Liam Brady, who played but was not fully fit. Another Irishman, DAVID O'LEARY, also started.

It was a hot day. Ipswich endured it better and deserved the victory. They won the battle in midfield, where Brian Talbot and John Wark ruled supreme.

PAUL MARINER was a constant menace and rattled Arsenal's crossbar.

Roger Osborne struck the winning goal, and immediately fell down exhausted and had to be helped from the field.

MICK MILLS was the happy chappie who carried away the trophy. And a year later he lifted this trophy, the European Cup Winners' Cup.

1979

It would forever be known as the 'Five-Minute Final' because most of the action was squeezed into those last dramatic minutes.

Not that the previous 85 minutes were that bad, but Arsenal seemed to be cruising to a deserved victory.

Who scored their first goal? BRIAN TALBOT said he did. After helping Ipswich in 1978, Talbot returned with his new team. Frank Stapleton also netted, and at 2-0

Arsenal sent on their substitute Steve Walford.

But first McQueen scored, 2-1. Then McILROY made it 2-2, and Walford hadn't even touched the ball.

United, still buzzing, switched off. LIAM BRADY, who'd had a nightmare in 1978, was fully fit this time and engineered the winner.

ALAN SUNDERLAND scored it, and then took off like a crazy man. It's a good job the gates were closed.

Wonderful Wembley moments

1979

We shall never know what would have happened if Brian Clough had become England's manager in 1977. The position suddenly became vacant after Don Revie's departure, and Clough was the 'people's choice' to succeed him. It didn't happen.

After Ron Greenwood had been asked to do the job on only a 'temporary arrangement', interviews were carried with six good men shortlisted for the position. Clough was one of those interviewed. But some high-up official at the FA, and probably more than one of them, thought that Clough would be too hot to handle. Perhaps they feared for their jobs.

Greenwood had done a good job in the meantime, leading England to an impressive win over Italy in a World Cup qualifier at Wembley, so he was given the position full time.

Two years later Wembley was again the venue for this Home International with Scotland.

TREVOR BROOKING is one of England's all-time legends. If he headed only one goal in his life, it had to be at Wembley. And it had to be the winning goal in an FA Cup Final, in 1980.

After bringing home an FA Cup winner's medal in 1977, STEVE COPPELL later went back to Wembley as manager of Crystal Palace in 1990. He played many times for England, and this was one of his best performances.

It was Ron Greenwood's good fortune to have both Kevin Keegan and Trevor Brooking at the top of their form together. As so often when coming to Wembley, Scotland raised their game, this being the one fixture above all others that they were desperate to win.

And throughout the first half they were definitely the better team, with Souness, Hartford and Wark winning the midfield, and Dalglish and Jordan causing panic among the England backs. Wark gave the visitors a deserved lead, and it would have been more except for Clemence's superb save from Jordan. This example seemed to inspire the rest of his team, and just before half-time Peter Barnes equalised with a well struck shot. It may have been undeserved, but it lifted England's spirits as they left the field at the interval.

On the hour England took the lead following a flowing move, at the end of which Wood couldn't hold the shot from Wilkins and Coppell swooped on the rebound. England's third goal was a classic, something like the blackboard on the opposite page shows, an old-fashioned wall pass, executed perfectly by the two best players of the time. Keegan ran on to Brooking's return pass and shot past Wood. It was, as they say, a game of two halves, and the transformation in England's display was extraordinary.

Glenn Hoddle was one of the most naturally gifted players of his generation. Although it was felt by some critics that his work rate was insufficient, he scored some quite memorable goals. Who can forget that amazing volley against Manchester United? We may forget the time and place, but we can still see that goal in our mind's eye.

He loved the big stage, and Wembley in particular. He has two FA Cup winner's medals, scoring against Queens Park Rangers in the drawn 1982 final and then the winner in the replay, from the penalty spot.

He later managed England with less success than was hoped for. Here's a reminder of his England debut as a player at Wembley stadium in 1979, and another exquisite goal.

PHIL THOMPSON captained England in this game. His most memorable Wembley evening was a European Cup victory with Liverpool in 1978.

They looked at RAY WILKINS and called him 'Butch'. This was one of his best England displays. And when they vote for the best FA Cup Final goals the one he scored against Brighton in 1983 is high on the list.

ENGLAND 2 BULGARIA 0

IT WAS TOO FOGGY TO PLAY THIS MATCH ON WEDNESDAY EVENING. LET'S HOPE ALL THE PLAYERS WERE TOLD...

HAVE WE KICKED OFF YET?

YESTERDAY WE COULD SEE WEMBLEY IN ALL ITS GLORY, SO THE GAME WENT AHEAD

I JUST WANT GO BACK TO MY ROOM...

DAVE WATSON, WHO STILL WOULD NOT WIN ANY BEAUTY CONTESTS, SCORED FOR ENGLAND SOON AFTER THE START.

FOR THE BULGARIAN GOALIE IT WAS AS IF THE FOG NEVER LIFTED.

NEVER MIND WHERE IT CAME FROM, JUST PICK IT OUT AND LET'S CARRY ON...

THE VISITORS CONCENTRATED ON DEFENCE, AND KEEPING THE SCORE DOWN.

BUT AFTER THAT, ENGLAND STRUGGLED TO FIND A WAY THROUGH...

GLENN HODDLE MADE HIS LONG-AWAITED ENGLAND DEBUT...

HE RAN...

HE PASSED...

HE JUMPED...

HE DID ALL THINGS WELL, EVEN WHEN HE WAS STANDING STILL.

HODDLE FINISHED OFF THE EVENING WITH A WONDERFUL PASS INTO BULGARIA'S NET FROM 20 YARDS

THEY MIGHT PICK ME AGAIN...

GLENN HODDLE HAS TO BE A REGULAR ENGLAND CHOICE FOR THE NEXT DECADE...

Unfortunately the day's delay in playing this match robbed England of the services of Kevin Keegan, who had to return to Germany because of commitments to his club, Hamburg.

So Kevin Reeves replaced him, winning his first cap. Glenn Hoddle, too, was pulling on an England shirt for the first time.

The fog had lifted, and 72,000 still managed to get into their places, and they saw England win comfortably and seal their place in the following year's European Championship finals. In the very first minute Dave Watson missed a good opportunity as England pressed Bulgaria right from the kick-off. Watson atoned for his miss a few minutes later, heading in from Hoddle's centre. After that it continued to be one-way traffic towards Bulgaria's goal, but their custodian Khristov made save after save to defy England. Viv Anderson, the first black footballer ever to play for England, was having a good game in front of the underworked Ray Clemence. And although Wilkins was particularly impressive in midfield, England simply couldn't add to their lead.

The second half was more of the same, but the fans had to wait until the 70th minute for the magic moment when Hoddle marked his debut with a goal. Taking a pass from Trevor Francis he side-footed it perfectly into the top corner of Bulgaria's goal from 20 yards.

In his first game wearing the captain's armband, Phil Thompson had led England to an impressive victory.

1983

In the first four FA Cup Finals after the war, the team who had the north dressing room lost, giving rise to the superstition that the south dressing room was the luckier one. It is certainly true that far more of the teams who have been allocated the southernmost room have ended up winners.

Here, on the next few pages, are some more finals from the 1980s and 1990s, chosen at random, but too many of them featuring Manchester United. In all but one of these the winners used the south dressing room. The exception was in 1987, when one of the finalists was Coventry City.

When the Coventry coach was on its way to Wembley, the driver had to stop and ask for directions. The club had never been there before. Nor any of the players, except for Cyrille Regis who'd had the very occasional outing with England. At the other end of the field Ray Clemence was making his sixth appearance in an FA Cup Final.

Spurs had been regular visitors. They saw Wembley as a friend. Five times they had been there since the war and five times they had been victorious. The cockerel would be crowing again, that was certain. The north Londoners were firm favourites. Coventry had probably made enquiries about an open-top bus on their return to the city, but more in hope than expectation.

Some of the club managers who had good memories of at least one Wembley occasion, BOB PAISLEY at Liverpool, TOMMY DOCHERTY at Manchester United, BOBBY ROBSON at Ipswich, RON ATKINSON at Manchester United and Aston Villa, Sir ALEX FERGUSON at Manchester United and ARSÈNE WENGER at Arsenal.

Manchester United were expected to win this, yet could so easily have been beaten. Already-relegated Brighton made nonsense of the gulf between themselves and their opponents in the First Division table, and helped to make this one of Wembley's more exciting and unpredictable finals.

Incessant rain before the match created a slippery surface which contributed to the fast exchanges. If Brighton missed the suspended Steve Foster, 20-year-old Gary Stevens rose to the occasion, defending and attacking with boundless energy.

Brighton led at half-time courtesy of Gordon Smith's header. Frank Stapleton, a scorer against United in an earlier cup final, this time got one for them to tie the game at 1-1. With 20 minutes to go Wilkins curled a delicious shot beyond Moseley's dive. That looked enough, and surely Ron Atkinson's men would go on to win. But the non-stop Stevens popped up with the equaliser three minutes from the end to take the game into extra time.

The drama wasn't over. As the cartoon relates, Smith had the chance, from Robinson's pass, to send Brighton fans into heaven. His shot was well struck and on target, but Bailey saved it. There have been far worse misses at Wembley, but none at a more opportune time. Brighton lost the replay, and Ron Atkinson went out and bought some more jewellery.

By now the old stadium was beginning to look rather decrepit. One frustrated spectator expressed his disgust.

'I learn that the 100th FA Cup Final was the first £2m football match to be staged in Britain. What an absolute disgrace that, even though the long-suffering and often maligned football fan is prepared to pay enormous prices to watch a game, he has to go to what must be the worst national stadium in Europe. Wembley, playing surface apart, is sadly lacking in decent facilities. I recently paid £8.50 to watch England play. As if it isn't bad enough watching England these days, I had to sit on a rotting plank and wade through overflowing sewage from the ancient sanitary accommodation to get there. The so-called refreshment box had to be seen to be believed. If the receipts from the final are £2m it's about time we had a stadium to be proud of.' But we would have to wait another 20 years for that.

Clement Freud, in one of his wonderful match reports, once wrote, 'At half-time the game's virginity was still intact.'

Instead he could easily have said that there was no score at half-time, but Clement was never so boring. Here, in the 1985 final, the game's virginity was still intact at full time, so into an extra half-hour we went. What we had seen was a first sending-off in an FA Cup Final. Was referee Peter Willis too hard on United's Kevin Moran as he tackled Everton's Peter Reid? Possibly so. Reid flew through the air with the greatest of ease, and Mr Willis pointed the Irishman towards the exit. A caution would have been enough. What the dismissal did was to galvanise United into rising up and beating Everton fairly and squarely, when they could have resigned themselves to defeat. They destroyed Everton's dreams of an historic treble, and did so with a goal of absolute beauty from Norman Whiteside. It came with ten minutes of extra time left, and was worthy of winning any final. There was very little to aim at, but Whiteside curled his shot around Van den Hauwe and beyond Southall and inside the post.

There is a rule that prevents a sent-off player from receiving his medal, but it is to be hoped that there will be a change of mind here. Moran deserves his medal. And so does Stapleton, who moved back from United's attack to fill Moran's position, and played magnificently.

There have not been many FA Cup Finals as good as this one, and once again it needed an extra half-hour before we knew the destiny of the trophy, and it did not go the way of the favourites. Spurs lost, but contributed much to a game that crackled and fizzed from the start when Clive Allen opened the scoring with a thumping header.

It was just as we expected. But Coventry were not going to lie down and be walked over. They had a plan. They would not have as much possession as Spurs, but when they did get the ball they struck swiftly and with good effect. Bennett's equaliser reminded Spurs that things would not be straightforward. Allen looked in vain for his 50th goal of the season. Mabbutt then scored the first of his two goals, this one at the right end. Always in the thick of the action, Mabbutt was also the victim of Kilcline's physical excess, and was lucky to be able to carry on. Once again the Sky Blues hit back. Sometimes we save our best moments for the big stage, the right place and time, and Houchen has probably never scored a more spectacular goal than this one.

By extra time Spurs had punched themselves out, and it was City who got the decider, albeit an own goal by the unfortunate Mabbutt. It was no consolation, but he was not the first man to score at both ends in an FA Cup Final.

1988

Liverpool were, beyond question, the English club side of the 1980s. Wembley was almost as familiar to them as Anfield. It was at Wembley that they won the Football League Cup in 1981 and they kept hold of it for the next three years. Here are a few of their main men of that decade.

JOHN BARNES, brilliant for club and for country.

ALAN HANSEN, a cool and polished defender who also played for Scotland at Wembley. Later, as a popular pundit, Hansen became infamous for his prophecy about Manchester United's 'kids'.

RONNIE WHELAN scored twice when Liverpool beat Spurs in the 1982 League Cup Final.

KENNY DALGLISH's favourite Wembley memory was scoring Liverpool's winner against Brugge in the European Cup Final in 1978, and leaping the advertising boards to celebrate with the fans.

But one day the all-conquering Liverpool met their match. The 'Crazy Gang' of Wimbledon, who rose out of nowhere to terrorise the old First Division, then went on to defeat Liverpool in the 1988 FA Cup Final.

It was as unlikely as any cup giant-killing, simply because it was Liverpool who were slain.

Sanchez headed the only goal from Wise's free

kick, and then Wimbledon chased and tackled for all they were worth.

You wouldn't want to meet VINNIE JONES on a dark night. And meeting him on the football field was no happy encounter either. He marked his man in more ways than one.

This wasn't the last success DENNIS WISE would have at Wembley. He would bring home two other FA Cup winner's medals playing for Chelsea.

Wimbledon's other hero was Dave Beasant, who saved Aldridge's penalty kick to preserve their lead.

JOHN ALDRIDGE learned that if Wembley knocked you down at one time, it could pick you up the next, as he would score the opening goal in the following year's final.

The two Merseyside giants, Liverpool and Everton, put together an FA Cup Final to savour. But for 89 minutes Liverpool were in total control. John Aldridge's early goal might have sparked an avalanche, so well were the red shirts moving, passing and opening up the Everton defence. But the Blues, and goalkeeper Southall in particular, would not submit.

Much as Liverpool were dominant, the second goal would not arrive, and all the time Everton were just one goal in arrears they believed they were in with a chance. Southall defied Aldridge, Beardsley and Barnes with save after save. At the other end of the field Liverpool's defence seemed like a safely padlocked door.

Everton's boss Colin Harvey sent on Stuart McCall as a reinforcement for his overworked defence. Kenny Dalglish responded by throwing substitute Ian Rush into the fray.

But Harvey's sub came up trumps first, as in the last 15 seconds of normal time McCall was in the right spot to stab in the equaliser. For 85 minutes Liverpool had led, comfortably. Now they had to do it all again in extra time.

It was Rush who restored the lead with a shot that even Southall couldn't reach. McCall then levelled the score again. Has Wembley ever had such an unlucky loser? For a loser he was, as Rush was there once again, this time with a header from a cross from Barnes, and there was no way back for the Toffeemen. Everton had done their best, but justice was served by the result.

Palace arrived at Wembley full of self-belief. Their FA Cup achievements had given them that, especially an entirely surprising semi-final victory over Liverpool.

Manchester United came to the final needing to win to be sure of keeping Alex Ferguson in a job. His tenure was so uncertain.

Palace's confidence looked completely justified when O'Reilly rose to head Barber's free kick past Jim Leighton. The United goalkeeper was to have an uncomfortable game. But the scores were levelled when McClair centred for Robson to head in at the other end.

After Mark Hughes had given United the lead in the second half, Steve Coppell decided it was time to send on substitute Ian Wright, who had broken a leg earlier in the year and had barely recovered. Immediately Wright burst through on to Bright's pass and slammed the ball past Leighton.

In extra time Wright found the net again after Leighton had flapped at a cross from Salako.

Underdogs Palace were ahead, and held on to their lead until seven minutes from time when Hughes got his second after Danny Wallace had put him through.

For the replay, Leighton was dropped and Les Sealey famously took his place and kept a clean sheet. The right place at the right time, Sealey had played only twice before for United. They won the replay at Wembley by the only goal, Lee Martin shooting past Nigel Martyn.

For the first time, a semi-final of the FA Cup was played at Wembley. The FA justified its decision to do this on the grounds that more fans would be able to attend. It was to begin a trend that saw Wembley host semi-finals for years ahead.

Spurs' victory over Arsenal featured a wonderful long-distance free kick by Gascoigne, and two goals from Lineker.

The final saw Gascoigne move from hero to zero, as he could so easily do. For his horrible first-minute tackle he could have been sent off, and it would have been better for him if he had. His next challenge on Gary Charles finished him once and for all. As the seriously injured Gascoigne was helped off, the free kick he had conceded was driven home by Stuart Pearce.

Referee Milford could also have dismissed Forest goalkeeper Crossley for his foul on Lineker. A penalty kick was awarded, but the usually deadly Lineker saw his shot saved.

Paul Stewart equalised in the second half, and once again extra time was needed to separate the winners from the losers. Des Walker, a rock in defence for both Forest and England, headed into his own net. Mabbutt, himself an own goal villain in a previous final, this time lifted the trophy.

This 113th FA Cup Final was not as one-sided as the scoreline would suggest. A stormy afternoon had been forecast for Wembley. We had the rain, but we were spared the thunder.

Only the atmosphere crackled with excitement as Chelsea took the game to their more illustrious rivals. United already had the Premier League championship trophy in their cabinet, but had been twice beaten by Chelsea, so they knew they were in for a battle. Having got the winning goal both times in the league, Peacock was very unlucky not to do the same again, as the drawing shows.

With an hour gone the final was still on a knife-edge when Newton sent Irwin tumbling with a mistimed tackle. Eric Cantona, the most celebrated performer of the day, made scoring look easy from the spot. If the award of the first penalty was clear-cut, the second was not so, Kanchelskis going to ground very easily from Sinclair's challenge. Again Mr Elleray pointed, and again Mr Cantona obliged.

Player-manager Glenn Hoddle sent himself on in an attempt to change things, but before he could get his knees warm Hughes added a third and Chelsea must have known that this simply was not going to be their day. But still they pushed forward, and but for Schmeichel's brilliance they would have had at least one goal. He saved well from Wise, Spencer and Peacock before substitute McClair tapped in United's fourth, unselfishly laid on by Ince. Sharpe came on, if only to add some glamour to the post-match photographs.

Bryan Robson, who would soon become manager of Middlesbrough, didn't feature.

'To leave him out was my hardest decision in management,' said Alex Ferguson.

1990

There are some players we wish we had seen more of at Wembley. Great club footballers, like Matt Le Tissier for example, never played in an FA Cup Final, and we can think of many others. Le Tissier did make a few fleeting appearances for England at Wembley – many as substitute – but he should have charmed the stadium more often with his extraordinary skills.

The debate about the great English maverick, of which Le Tissier was one, goes back to the days of Len Shackleton and Stan Bowles and such like. Alan Hudson was another. None of them won as many caps as they should have, probably because they were free range, and didn't fit into any system.

Paul Gascoigne was similar. This was his breakthrough game as England were preparing for another World Cup. Should he go, or should he not? This performance against Czechoslovakia convinced Bobby Robson that he could not go to Italy without Gazza.

This may have been
Gazza's match, but STEVE
BULL did his Wembley bit
with two exquisitely taken goals.

As he readily admits, GARY LINEKER
got most of his goals from very close range.
But get them he did, for he was the
expert finisher for club and for
country. He collected his FA Cup
winner's medal for Spurs in 1991.

This was Paul Gascoigne's match from beginning to end. England had found a new star. That was the general verdict after a fine victory over another of the World Cup favourites. In only his second full game for his country, Gascoigne staged a one-man show that had Wembley buzzing. It was such a pity that only 21,000 turned up to see it.

England made a shocking start, conceding a goal early on to the eager Czechs. At this point the home team were looking for some inspiration, and Gascoigne provided it, sending a superb pass to Steve Bull who finished emphatically. Soon England were ahead, Stuart Pearce scoring following a corner kick by Gascoigne, who seemed to be involved in everything. West Ham's Ludo Miklosko was in goal for Czechoslovakia, and he must have seen Gascoigne before. But Ludo had no chance of saving Bull's thumping header from another pin-point cross by you-know-who. With ten minutes to go the lively Czechs reduced England's lead and there were a few nervous minutes before Gascoigne provided the best moment of the evening. He sped through the visitors' defence before crashing his shot into the roof of Miklosko's net.

Gascoigne had written his name on to Bobby Robson's shortlist for Italia 90.

1996

As the 20th century drew nearer to its close, mankind was able to understand most things. In the 50 years since the end of the Second World War, we had advanced so much in knowledge and figuring things out. Looking through a microscope, man had seen the structure of the atom, and through a telescope had got to grips with the formation of outer space. And computers were with us, and a whole new world of information technology was beginning to open up. Based on a few fossilised bones over two million years old, we knew what a dinosaur looked like.

But we were utterly clueless about the workings of Paul Gascoigne. We got used to his antics, and just shook our heads. He had received heavy criticism in the press for his childish behaviour on England's team-building exercise in Hong Kong, and some had called for England to cast him aside. But put a football at his feet, and he could do extraordinary things that nobody else could. And once again, he did.

ALLY McCOIST played for Scotland against England at Wembley in Euro 96. Statistic alert! McCoist scored no less than 355 goals for Rangers in a glittering career.

Another legendary member of the Scotland team that day was ANDY GORAM. In a poll of Rangers fans Goram was voted 'best-ever goalkeeper'.

When England played Spain in the quarter-finals, unusually for them they won the game after a penalty shoot-out. Goalkeeper DAVID SEAMAN was their hero that afternoon, saving two Spanish penalties.

STUART PEARCE scored with his penalty in that shoot-out, finally putting to bed his miss from the spot in Italia 90.

Arsenal fans remember DENNIS BERGKAMP with much affection. He was one of the stars of a very talented Dutch team.

So was goalkeeper EDWIN VAN DER SAR. But he was powerless to stop England's goal rush at Wembley.

PATRICK KLUIVERT's goal was the only blemish on England's performance. Sadly, it eliminated the Scots.

JURGEN KLINSMANN is well remembered for a wonderful season with Spurs. Rightly or wrongly he had a reputation as a 'diver'. But he was a winner here with Germany.

GARY McALLISTER had a long and great career with several clubs, and with Scotland. But oh, that penalty miss.

PATRIK BERGER scored for the Czechs in the final at Wembley, but was on the losing side. Later in the year he joined Liverpool.

England, managed by Terry Venables, had made a slow start to the tournament, and were held to an undistinguished draw by Switzerland in their opening match. Gascoigne answered his critics in the best possible manner. His moment didn't arrive until late in the game with Scotland. Before that these close rivals had struggled to get going, but when Alan Shearer headed in Gary Neville's cross early in the second half, all seemed set fair for an England win.

But Scotland refused to go down without a fight, and Durie forced a good save from Seaman.

A few minutes later the England goalkeeper was tested to the full when he had to face a penalty, Durie having been brought down by Adams. As McAllister began his run-up, the ball appeared to move slightly from the spot. Uri Geller later claimed the credit. McAllister still struck his shot well, but Seaman threw up his arm and saved.

Scotland had no time to regret the miss before Gascoigne again took centre stage. He collected Anderton's pass, flicked the ball over Hendry, ran around him and volleyed it crisply past Goram in a moment of sheer brilliance.

The dentist's chair mimicry which followed is best forgotten, however.

This was one of the old country's greatest performances. Holland had frequently got the better of England in the past, and 1993 was still fresh in our memories as the Koeman brothers, and some questionable refereeing, effectively ended Graham Taylor's reign as manager. 'Your mate has just lost me my job,' said Taylor to a linesman.

All was forgotten as the Dutchmen were played off the park. Shearer got the first goal from the penalty spot, and England could have been further ahead at half-time. In the second half they touched perfection as first Sheringham headed in from a corner, and then, after a delightful move involving McManaman, Gascoigne and Sheringham, Shearer slammed in number three. It was Sheringham again who bagged the fourth after van der Sar failed to hold on to Anderton's scorching shot.

The only sad moment came just before the end when Kluivert netted for Holland, ending Scotland's hopes of progressing.

'Football is a simple game: 22 men chase a ball for 90 minutes and, at the end, the Germans win,' said Gary Lineker.

England's bandwagon came to a shocking halt as Germany once again got the better of the hosts to reach the final of the European Championship.

England appeared to be on the crest of a wave after their splendid display against Holland, which they took into their victory on penalties against Spain in the quarter-finals, and that confidence grew some more when Shearer headed them into a third-minute lead. Wembley, already throbbing with passion and patriotism, went wild. But did England score too early? Germany soon levelled with a suspiciously offside goal, and that was the end of the scoring in the first 90 minutes, although both sides had their opportunities to win.

In extra time the English came agonisingly close when Anderton struck a post and when from three yards out Gascoigne just failed to connect with Shearer's cross.

Once again England and Germany would have to be separated by penalties. It was a shoot-out of serious quality as both teams scored with all five of their kicks. Then Southgate's shot was saved, and as we knew he would Andreas Moller did his bit to finally end England's hopes of reaching the final. It had been a gallant attempt, but once again it was doomed to failure.

Germany – of course they did – went on to lift the trophy.

ROBERTO DI MATTEO scored in two FA Cup Finals for Chelsea. His thunderous opener against Middlesbrough in 1997 was the fastest cup final goal ever. And his winner against Villa in 2000 was the last goal in a final at the old Wembley.

GIANFRANCO ZOLA also starred for Chelsea in that final. It was from his free kick that the winning goal came.

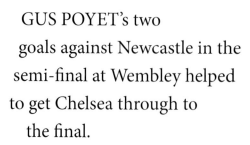

GUS POYET's two goals against Newcastle in the semi-final at Wembley helped to get Chelsea through to the final.

A loser that day was DION DUBLIN. Ten years earlier Dublin had got the first-ever goal in a play-off final, for Cambridge United. It is a place in the record books that nobody can take away.

Last at the old, first at the new. When the FA Cup Final returned to Wembley in 2007 DIDIER DROGBA got the first goal in a final at the new stadium, for Chelsea against Manchester United.

MICHAEL OWEN scored lots of goals for England, and was the first player to score for his country at both Wembleys.

Here, too, are WAYNE ROONEY, DAVID BECKHAM and STEVEN GERRARD, who all graced Wembley with their skills and goalscoring at the turn of the millennium.

The New Wembley Stadium

The FA Challenge Trophy, the Challenge Vase, the Auto Windscreens Shield. Because some less prestigious knock-out competitions end with a final showdown at Wembley, fans of the most unlikely teams from little towns have known the joy of a day out at Wembley, and coming home with a win and a smile. Supporters of Colne Dynamos, Billericay Town and Bishop's Stortford all know what it's like, whilst at the time of writing this neither Bournemouth, Fulham nor Middlesbrough have ever won at Wembley. Nor have Brighton.

Then there are the divisional play-offs. The annual match at Wembley to decide which of the two teams goes into the Premier League is the most money-spinning game of the season.

Leicester City were always the bridesmaids at Wembley, losing in six finals, before finally in 1994 winning a play-off against Derby County. Similarly Preston North End, as this cartoonist well knows, had to experience several heartbreaks here before this win in 2015. But when it finally happens Wembley becomes your friend, and on that day there is nowhere else that you would rather be. So this cartoon is included just to please him.

But first a recent international between the old foes, and an exciting FA Cup Final. Arsenal have not featured very much in this book, which is quite unfair because they have been to both Wembley stadiums more than any other club side.

So here they are winning the cup once again.

2013

This was a thrilling encounter, the kind of end-to-end battle that England v Scotland matches ought to be. Neither side deserved to lose, but Scotland were beaten after twice being ahead, and the goal that consigned them to defeat will long be remembered by the man who scored it.

But first let's set the scene. Roy Hodgson's team needed a stern test before the upcoming World Cup qualifiers, and Scotland would be the team to give them that. For a long time England were the second best team on view, and chasing the game. Scotland scored first.

Morrison's shot was hard and low, through a crowd of players, but Hart should have saved it.

England's moments of brilliance were few and far between, but Walcott equalised with a left foot shot after being cleverly sent through by Cleverley.

In the second half Scotland regained the initiative, and the lead. It was vintage Kenny Miller as he took down Hutton's cross, dummied Cahill brilliantly, and drilled his shot beyond Hart.

England needed to respond quickly, which they did. Four minutes later Welbeck headed in Gerrard's free kick. The excitement rose a notch or two.

The moment of romance arrived with 20 minutes left, when Roy Hodgson sent on Rickie Lambert for his first taste of international football. Leighton Baines swung in a corner kick and Lambert rose majestically to head into the top corner, leaving McGregor helpless and scoring with his first touch of the ball in an England shirt.

Arsenal made an unbelievably bad start, going two goals down before making any impact at all. Shots from James Chester and Curtis Davies gave Hull City, the underdogs, a flying start. The contrast on the faces of the two managers spoke volumes. Arsene Wenger would have subsituted his whole team, while Steve Bruce clearly couldn't believe his own eyes. And if his boy's header had not been headed off the line, there would have been absolutely no way back for the Gunners.

But 2-0, as they say, is a vulnerable scoreline. Cazorla looped a brilliant free kick past McGregor, and Arsenal were able to go in at half-time with some hope. City clung on to their lead for a long time, chasing, tackling and throwing their bodies in Arsenal's way. Just as it began to look like being City's day Laurent Koscielny popped up in the opposition's goal area, as he often does. 2-2, and extra time, then. Aaron Ramsey, whose injury had hit Arsenal so seriously in the latter part of the season, drove in the winner with ten minutes left. Arsenal survived a few anxious moments as Hull fought to the finish, and Aluko came squeakingly close to equalising.

Referee Lee Probert's final whistle signalled a first FA Cup win for the Gunners at the new Wembley, and it was the 11th time they had lifted the old trophy.

It is said that winning promotion at Wembley is the best way to go up.

After so much heartache due to nine failed play-off attempts, Preston North End and their long-suffering supporters finally had a day to enjoy as their team won its way back into the Championship.

There were jubilant scenes in the west side of the stadium almost from the first whistle, as Beckford's second minute strike was quickly added to by Huntington's close-range finish. Both goals were set up by Gallagher's dead-ball precision.

Swindon then enjoyed a spell of pressure which almost resulted in a goal, Michael Smith's header missing by inches. It was as close as it got. From the goal kick Garner helped the ball on to Beckford, who turned his marker around before curling a delightful left-footer into the corner of Town's net.

The second half was a formality as Beckford completed his hat-trick, before being taken off with the cheers of the North End fans ringing in his ears. It was against this background of noise that skipper Tom Clarke lifted the trophy a few minutes later. At last the fans knew what it was like to win here.

This scene is repeated at all play-off finals, every year.

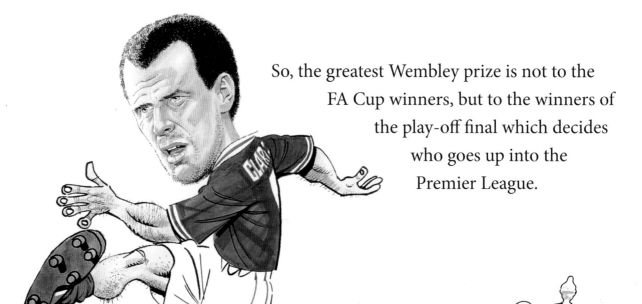

So, the greatest Wembley prize is not to the FA Cup winners, but to the winners of the play-off final which decides who goes up into the Premier League.

In 1996 Leicester City came from behind to beat Crystal Palace with STEVE CLARIDGE scoring their winner in the last seconds of extra time.

And the most memorable of these games was in 1998. Sunderland, the favourites, kept taking the lead against Charlton Athletic, but time and again CLIVE MENDONCA drew the Addicks level again. 4-4, after extra time, and into a penalty shoot-out where, after 13 successful spot-kicks goalkeeper Sasa Ilic became Charlton's second hero of the day, saving and sending them upwards.

We all love CHRIS KAMARA, don't we? He is the roving match reporter who one day didn't notice that a player had been sent for an early bath.

Jeff Stelling cut to him and said, 'There's been a sending off at Portsmouth. Who for? Chris Kamara?'

Kamara replied, 'I don't know, Jeff. Has there? I must have missed that.'

Kamara was a useful player in his day, with several clubs, and had his day at Wembley in 1996 when, as manager of Bradford City, he saw them to victory in the Second Division play-off final.

'Unbelievable, Jeff.'

When he stepped on to the Wembley grass as manager of Swindon Town in 1990, OSSIE ARDILES must have thought back to his first appearances at the stadium as a player for Spurs in 1983, when it took two games to dispose of Manchester City.

So when Swindon won their play-off final, Ossie would be looking forward to management in the First Division the following season. But a few weeks later Swindon were found guilty of 'financial irregularities' and made to stay in the Second Division. Sunderland were promoted instead.

2019

Manchester City's previous FA Cup Final at Wembley had ended in a shock defeat, Wigan scoring the only goal in the dying moments of the game. Few people expected that one, least of all their manager Roberto Mancini, who was promptly sacked. His replacement, Manuel Pellegrini, didn't last either. City continued to win the occasional trophy, but that wasn't good enough for their owners. So in came Pep Guardiola in 2016.

Wembley has been very kind to the Sky Blues since then. At the time of writing they have kept the Football League Cup in their cabinet for the last three years. So the new stadium has become as familiar to City's fans as their own backyard.

Watford had done very well to reach the FA Cup Final, but held no fears for Pep's people.

SERGIO AGUERO had scored in all three of those Football League Cup Final triumphs, so Wembley had seen the very best of City's star striker. Despite being their all-time leading goalscorer, he was on the substitutes' bench for this final.

Young PHIL FODEN was on the bench, too. He had been named man of the match following a great contribution to City's Football League Cup victory a few weeks earlier. Foden is one of England's most promising players, and opened his international account with two goals against Iceland at Wembley in 2020.

Luther Blissett, a former Watford player, and Tony Book, the City captain when they won the FA Cup in 1969, brought out the trophy before the game.

The Wembley story is sprinkled with great goals, and also some missed opportunities. Watford had an early chance, but muffed it. City boss Pep Guardiola admitted, 'If Watford had scored then, it would have been harder for us.'

Watford also appealed for a penalty when the ball struck Vincent Kompany on the arm, but after consulting VAR, referee Kevin Friend was not their friend, and refused their claims.

After David Silva drew first blood midway through the first half, it was plain sailing for City. A 2-0 half-time lead was doubled and then trebled, and the Hornets must have been relieved to hear the final whistle.

Kevin de Bruyne, scorer of the third goal, was named man of the match, and Kompany, City's captain, announced that this had been his last game for the club and that he was returning to Belgium to become player-manager of Anderlecht.

Wembley had never before witnessed a six-goal margin in an FA Cup Final.

The Women's FA Cup Final 2020

This was how cup finals were meant to be; the two best teams in the land, going at each other, all out attack and blow the consequences, a feast of football. The Wembley showpiece, worthy of the venue.

Sadly, some of our men's finals have been like cold porridge, with the teams too defence-minded and afraid to take risks. A let-down for a great stadium.

Not so with the ladies, and this final was full of good football. It was skilful and exciting, and compared favourably with anything that had been served up before. We were treated to 90 minutes of attractive running, passing, shooting and saving – and then some more, as the game moved into extra time, still on a knife-edge.

Although it deserved an audience, the match was played without any fans because of the ongoing coronavirus restrictions.

United States midfielder Sam Mewis had headed City in front and, as the cartoon shows, Val Gauvin had levelled for Everton with another header.

After the added half-hour City narrowly emerged as winners with late goals from Georgia Stanway and Janine Beckie, and so carried off the Cup for the third time.

A few England v Scotland games have been remembered in these pages, but few have been so eagerly anticipated as the encounter at Wembley in Euro 2021. The crowds of conflicting supporters may be missing, but never the fervour.

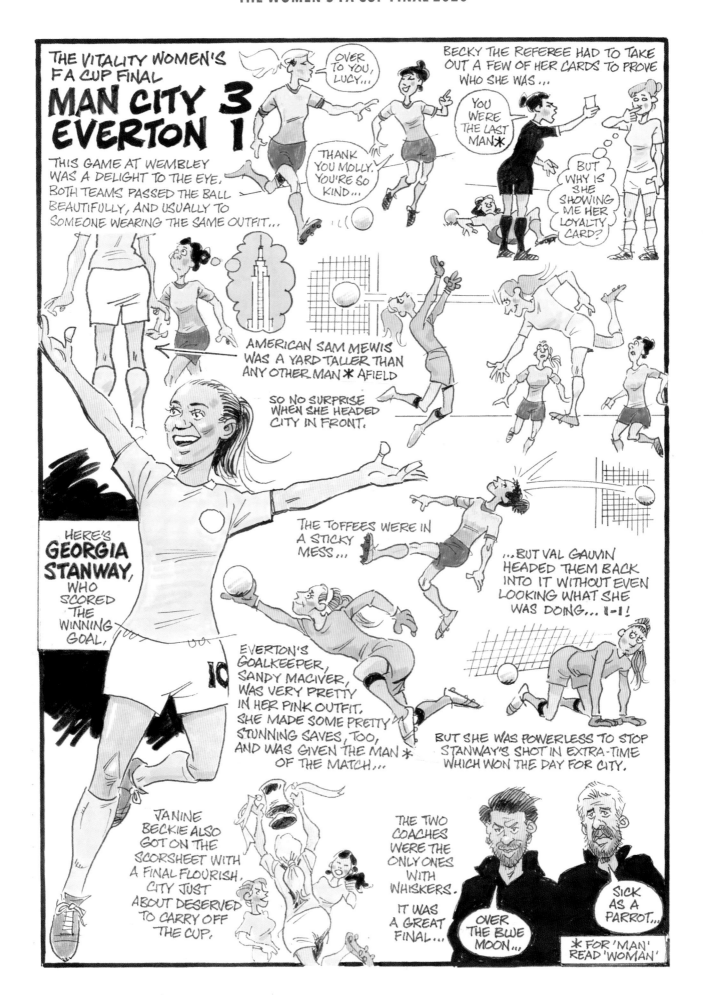

Twice in 2019 HARRY KANE walked off the Wembley pitch clutching the match ball after registering hat-tricks for England, against Bulgaria and against Montenegro. His fans will be hoping for the same again.

MARCUS RASHFORD is no stranger to Wembley, with several international appearances, and goals. Shortly after helping Manchester United to win the FA Cup here in 2016 he became his country's youngest goalscorer on his England debut.

JACK GREALISH led Villa to a play-off victory over Derby County at Wembley in 2019. A year later Jack pulled on the England shirt for his first full international start. Many others will follow, for certain.

Wembley will touch someone on the shoulder and turn him into England's next superhero.

HARRY MAGUIRE's chief job is to help to stop the other team from scoring. But his chief delight is to trot upfield and get himself on the scoresheet, as he did for his country against the Republic of Ireland at Wembley in 2020.

Gareth Southgate has a wealth of young talent to choose from. Phil Foden might be the one to end England's long years of hurt.

The inspiration might come from Chelsea's MASON MOUNT. He scored twice for England at Wembley in 2020, against Belgium and Iceland.

Leicester's JAMES MADDISON, whose club form has been so impressive, is another of the country's exciting rising stars.

But England will know that there is some frightening talent in the Scotland line-up as well. Liverpool's ANDREW ROBERTSON, a fine attacking full-back.

Here, too, is RYAN CHRISTIE of Celtic, a foe to be reckoned with.

Acknowledgements

I would like to thank more than a few people who have helped me along the way.

I thank my father and mother, who blessed me with some talent and supported me when I wanted to take a different career path to the one they intended for me.

I thank the teachers at my schools for encouraging me to draw whenever the urge came.

I thank the great Frank Hampson who I saw, in Southport, doing his first drawings of Dan Dare, Pilot of the Future. This first put the idea into my 11-year-old head that I wanted to do comics.

I thank my lecturers at art college who did their best to teach me how to draw.

I thank the sports editor of my local newspaper who first gave me a chance to see my scribblings in print.

I thank the editors of various comics, newspapers and books who also took a chance on me.

I thank all those artists and cartoonists who inspired me, from Ronald Searle and his Molesworth drawings, onwards.

I thank all the comedians who have made me laugh, and all the sportsmen and sportswomen who have thrilled me.

I thank my two wives who, in turn, have had to put up with me waking up in the middle of the night to jot down an idea before the inspiration fled away.

I'd like to thank Paul, Jane, Gareth, Dean, Graham and Duncan at Pitch Publishing for putting this book together.

Finally, I thank you for buying this book.

Bob Bond is a Lancastrian, but escaped some time ago to set up home on the South Coast. He began sketching soccer stories 60 years ago for various children's comics, and has been drawing footballers ever since for books, magazines and newspapers. Bob's wife thinks he's retired, but while she's out shopping he sneaks back into his studio and still draws cartoons for several publications. He has written and drawn comic strip histories of some of the bigger English clubs. Because Bob still follows Preston North End from afar, he looks older than he really is. He also suffers from an inferiority complex, having a son who is a much more talented artist than himself.

Also available at all good book stores

9781785316333

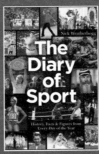

9781785316289

9781785315510

9781785316388

9781785316869

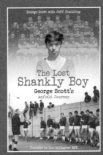

9781785316784

9781785316838

9781785316906

9781785316326